Hydro Gardens

The Techno Grow

tom flowers

CORRESPONDENCE TO:
Flowers Publishing Company
Box 5666
Berkeley, CA 94705
fax 510 595 3779

Book and Cover Design:
Pepper Design Studio

Photography by:
Tom Flowers & Larry Utley
(except where noted)

Cover Photography:
Tom Flowers

Edited by:
Dana Cannazopolous

This book is for informational purposes only.

DISTRIBUTED BY:

USA & Canada
Publishers Group West
tel: 800 788 3123
fax: 510 658 3834

United Kingdom
Avalon
tel: (01) 705 293 673
fax: (01) 705 780 444

Australia
Agung Trading Company
tel: (06) 280 7266
fax: (06) 280 7367

Netherlands
Sensi Seed b.v.
tel: (010) 477 3033
fax: (010) 477 8893

Norway
Scorpious Imports
tel: (47) 223 740 41
fax: (47) 223 731 36

ISBN # 0-9647946-3-2

Table of Contents

Marijuana Hydro Gardens
The Techno Grow

by Tom Flowers

They had a garden
Day was night
By the freeway
In electric light

PREFACE

I was going to use the term hydroponics in the title of this manual, but I didn't want to scare people off. Something in that term means fussy, cranky systems that annoy even people interested in horticulture. In the past, hydroponics systems often were indeed unreliable and complicated. Nobody wants to set up a growing system so complex it takes more time to use than picking up a watering can and servicing your plants.

For this reason, I decided to loose the "ponics" in hydroponics, and go with the term "hydro" - so aqueous and drenched. Basically, we are going to be exploring fancy ways of delivering life-sustaining water to marijuana. All other facets of growing marijuana will also be looked at, of course, but automated watering is the focus of this book.

It is no secret that hydro gardening systems have become easy to set up. Unlike just a few years ago, they are very dependable, and relatively inexpensive. Indoor garden stores have got the message, and developed the equipment growers want. It's no great revelation that marijuana, America's biggest cash crop, has driven many of the advances in this system of horticulture.

Hydro growing systems, once the domain of the technologically adept, are now available to anyone. It may take a little longer to set up and grow in this way, but the systems will quickly pay back the time as they operate. Besides automation and dependability, hydro systems take much of the guesswork out of growing, making successful crops much more likely.

Though I can simplify growing techniques so that almost anyone can set up an automated grow, I can't change the dim view America has concerning marijuana cultivation. It is safe to say growers won't be entering their prize plants in the county fair any time soon. As a matter of fact, using high tech gardening in the growing of marijuana is often used to prove professionalism and enhance punishment.

Nearly 700,000 people are arrested each year for using, growing or selling marijuana. Politicians are falling all over each other to give heavy prison sentences to people involved with this herb. This is what you will be up against if you decide to grow marijuana.

FOREWORD

Hydro Made Easy

The last few years have seen a radical improvement in automated and semi-automated growing systems. Many of these systems seem perfectly designed for growing marijuana. They are easy to set up, reliable, and with a small investment, cultivators can harvest marijuana year round. Six crops a year under lights is not unusual.

Hydro gardening could be defined, broadly, as the growing of plants under constant optimum conditions. Many plants, including marijuana, grow best in a nutrient-rich, slightly acidic, moist growing medium that holds lots of air for healthy roots. Marijuana also likes a warm growing environment surrounded by air containing high levels of carbon dioxide, moderate humidity, and high intensity light. The indoor grower can easily control all of these conditions.

Automated greenhouse grows can be set up in a fashion similar to those used by cultivators growing indoors under lights. Outdoor cultivators cannot totally control growing conditions in the same way as the indoor grower. Still, outdoor growers often use many growing techniques, which might be considered hydro. These include: automated watering systems, time-released fertilizers, and conditioned soil.

How much automation is used in growing marijuana is really up to the grower. Systems vary from passive systems with no moving parts, to active systems that use timers, pumps, reservoirs, and other equipment. Organic growing methods can also be incorporated into automated hydro systems.

I have attempted to set up this book so growers can take from it as much, or as little as they want to know.

I have tried to simplify methods of setting up basic automated systems before including non-essential, but useful, technical information.

None of this is rocket science. In many respects, the popular automated systems are similar to each other. Once the basics are understood, a grower can easily change from one system to another by purchasing a few different parts.

It is important to realize that marijuana grows well within relatively wide parameters. With a basic knowledge of what makes marijuana thrive, almost anyone can devise a system that meets his or her needs.

This manual takes a "hands on" approach as to how hydro marijuana is grown indoors, in greenhouses, or in the great outdoors. Very little is left to theory or lore. Only techniques shown to reliably produce prime marijuana are evaluated.

Chapter 1

Marijuana Hydro Indoors

The exact equipment needed to set up a hydro unit depends, of course, on the kind of system you chose. There are four kinds of active systems in common use by indoor marijuana cultivators including ebb & flow (flood & drain), drip (modified), aeroponics, and nutrient film.

These systems are called active because they all use an electric pump to move nutrient-rich water from a reservoir to the plants through plastic tubing. Most often the systems are re-circulating; excess water is returned to the reservoir and reused. Each system does have distinct differences, but the basic hydro units all automate the watering and feeding of marijuana plants.

Growers who want to use any active hydro unit should check out the electrical system first. The place to start building the system is at the electrical box. Because hydro systems use both electricity and water, caution should be used in the set-up of these systems. Electrical systems must have the capacity to handle the power required, which is a significant amount when electric lights are used to grow the plants.

The one thousand-watt high-pressure sodium lamp, for example, is often used in growing marijuana. It consumes about 10 Amps of electricity. When you consider the pumps, timers, light movers, fans, and other equipment, which will also draw electric current, each thousand-watt system will bring the typical 15 amp circuit breaker within 80% of its capacity. This is a safe margin, and will prevent the electric lines from overheating. If you don't have 15 amps to use solely for growing, smaller wattage lights should be used. High-pressure sodium lights are also available in 600, 400 and 250-watt models.

The ground fault circuit interrupter replaces a regular grounded wall plug, and prevents shocks.

Electrical systems that are overloaded burn fuses or shut off circuit breakers frequently. A competent electrician should be consulted if the electrical system is not adequate. Never replace the fuse or breaker with one of higher amperage rating, such as a 15-amp fuse with a 20-amp fuse. This could cause your electrical wiring to overheat, leading to the potential of fire.

In addition, the electrical system should be grounded. The ground line is the third wire in modern electric systems. It is meant to filter excess current from faulty equipment into the ground. In addition, ground lines tend to turn off electrical systems when a short circuit occurs, by tripping the circuit breaker. Electrical systems without ground lines are usually older, and should not be considered for projects that are going to use a lot of electricity. A ground line is also necessary for the installation of a device (a ground fault circuit interrupter) that makes hydroponic equipment much safer to use.

The ground fault circuit interrupter is a device that fits in place of a regular electric outlet, and is used in places like kitchens and bathrooms, where water and electric appliances could come in contact. It shuts down the electric circuit immediately when it detects current flowing to ground, as happens in a short circuit. Ground fault circuit interrupters are meant to be lifesavers, reducing the likelihood of shock or electrocution from malfunctioning electrical systems. This device is inexpensive ($20), easy to install, and should be considered a must for indoor marijuana growers, especially those using hydro systems.

Money spent to upgrade an electrical system is well worth the peace of mind of operating a safe and reliable system. Remember these essential safety rules:

1. The power should be shut off when the system is serviced.
2. Position electrical equipment to prevent it from coming into contact with water.

Make 'safety first' your mantra.

Once you're sure your electrical system is adequate you can begin to consider which system you intend to use. A short list of the parts needed to set up an indoor hydro system will include much of the following:

THE PARTS FOR HYDRO .... NOTES
Electric Grow Lights
Ground Fault Circuit Interrupter
Table and Tray .... for ebb & flow and drip
                                        systems
Grow Tubes .... for aeroponic, nutrient
                                        film or drip systems
2 Timers .... one for the lights & a
                                        digital one for the pump
Power Strip
Pump with 1/2 inch nipple .... 10-15 gallon per minute
                                        (gpm)
Reservoir & Hose
1/2 inch Plastic Tubing .... Spaghetti lines for drip &
                                        aeroponics
Misters for aeroponics
Fans & Vents
Temperature/Humidity Gauge
Water Source
Negative Ion Generator
Mylar or Reflective Material

GROWING NEEDS
Fertilizer
Growing Media & Containers ..... if needed
Dissolved Solids & pH Meters
Plant Supports
Marijuana Seeds or Clones

HIGH TECH
Carbon Dioxide
Dehumidifier
Air Conditioner
Power Washer
Sensors

Once you are aware of the gizmos needed to set up an active hydro system, the time has arrived to determine which system you want. We will take a brief look at each kind of system, and how the parts fit together to make them work.

Ebb & Flow (Flood & Drain)

The ebb & flow system, once the clunker of the hydroponic world, has gotten a new lease on life. This is because of new equipment, such as digital timers, that let the grower strictly control the watering cycle, and also how these systems are currently set up and used. The new versions of the ebb & flow system are the winners in the hydro world in terms of dependability and ease of operation.

A tray with six-inch sides is placed on a table high enough for a reservoir to fit under. The reservoir holds water and nutrients, which are pumped up to the table through 1/2 inch plastic pipe. The pump is connected to one end of the pipe and placed at the bottom of the reservoir. The other end of the pipe is connected, with an adapter, to the bottom of the table. The pipe is used both to flood the tray, and to return excess nutrient solution back to the reservoir at the end of the watering cycle.

The pump is plugged into and controlled with a digital timer. These timers let the grower use short watering cycles of as little as one minute, up to twelve times a day. Growers commonly use several daily watering cycles of three to four minutes, especially when plants get large. Digital timers are the heart of the ebb & flow system. They are easy to program and very dependable. They turn on the pump, which floods the tray with water up to several inches deep, and then turn it off.

The growing media that can be used with the ebb & flow system can be as simple as four-inch rockwool cubes. One-gallon plastic containers filled with a reasonably absorbent medium, such as volcanic rock mixed with vermiculite, can also be used. If containers are used, try to get squat pots, which are wider rather than having high sides.

Ebb & Flow

This makes it easier to saturate the media in the container during the flood cycle. Because of the ease of set-up and long term dependability, ebb & flow systems have no downside, except for the potential for over-watering. For a hands-on look at the ebb & flow system in operation see chapter 6: Marijuana On Line

Drip Systems (modified)

The drip system is set up in a manner similar to the ebb & flow system, usually with a table and tray elevated above a reservoir. Drip systems can also be used with grow tubes.

In drip systems, a hole is drilled in the tray and 1/2 inch plastic tubing is run from the pump up into the tray. The pipe is capped at the end. It is used as a header to which a spaghetti line (thin plastic tubing) is connected and run to each marijuana plant. Up to 25 plants can be serviced from a single header.

The drip system is modified in that marijuana cultivators seldom use the drip emitters, which can be connected to the spaghetti line. The drip emitter limits the flow of water and nutrients, and frequently clogs up. Without emitters, drip systems are very dependable.

Watering cycles are controlled with a digital timer. The timer turns on the pump delivering nutrient solution to the plants through a spaghetti line connected to each container. The timing of the watering cycles is very variable, but is often programmed to run mostly while the lights are on.

Drip System

Excess water is returned to the reservoir by drilling a small 1/8 inch hole in tray right next to where the 1/2 inch header pipe enters the tray. Some water will also run down the 1/2 inch pipe. The reservoir is positioned to collect this excess water.

Modified drip systems have few downsides. A drip system can accommodate many kinds of growing media, for example, simply by adjusting the watering cycle. Almost any media capable of holding some water can be used. With the digital timer the marijuana can be watered several times a day. Or, if a water-holding medium is used, the plants can be watered only once every other day. Plant size and growing media determine how much nutrient solution the marijuana will draw. The digital timer can easily be programmed for just about any situation.

Modified drip systems are also versatile in that the marijuana plants can be moved around on the trays to make the most of available light, and avoid unproductive spots in the grow space.

Aeroponics

If you love to tinker, an aeroponic system might be for you. With these systems the roots of the marijuana plants are constantly drenched in nutrient solution with a misting device. The misters use water pressure to operate. Nutrient solution is pumped up from the reservoir and delivered to the plant's roots through the misters.

Aeroponics is said to be the fastest producing of the hydroponic growing systems because so much air, water and nutrient is delivered to the roots of the plant. However, the advantages of this system can be easily be defeated by one thing or another.

A typical aeroponic system is set up in 6 inch grow tubes drilled at regular intervals (usually 1 foot) to hold a small growing container. The container is made of a mesh material that water and roots can penetrate. Small amounts of growing media such as volcanic rock or ceramic beads are typically used. Because the containers are usually small the marijuana will need additional support to hold the plants in an upright position. Specially designed clips are available for this purpose. Because of the need for special parts, growers considering an aeroponic system, might also consider a "ready made" system.

Water moves from a reservoir by pump through 1/2 inch pipe up to the grow tubes. The pipe goes through the tube and is capped at the end. Small holes are punched into the pipe under each container, and a mister, which delivers a fine spray, is snapped into it. The grow tubes are set up at a slight angle so excess water is returned to the reservoir by gravity, through more 1/2 inch plastic pipe. Several grow tubes can be connected into this drainage system, which re-circulates the nutrient solution.

Aeroponic systems are available in kits, and if you really want to use one, this may be the way to go. Hunting up parts for a grower-designed aeroponic hydro system can be difficult. Take the critical part, the mister, for example. They are made by several manufacturers and operate best under set conditions like a specific water pressure. Kits are more likely to match compatible parts.

I won't kid you though; even when set up right, aeroponic systems can be cantankerous in operation. The list of what can go wrong is long. A higher capacity pump (50 gallons per minute) is often used for a small aeroponic system, for example, than would be used with a drip or flood system (10-15 gallons per minute). With higher water pressure the possibility of leaks increases. Also, because small amounts of growing media are used in most aeroponic set ups, the pumping system is operating most of the time. Over time, this increases the likelihood of a part failing, as compared to a system that runs briefly at intervals.

As was mentioned, the misters are the part of the system most likely to fail, since they tend to clog up. Filtering the water and nutrients as it returns to the reservoir helps to keep the solution free of debris and keep clogged misters to a minimum. Even so the large root systems marijuana develops under aeroponics assures a constant flow of debris as small pieces of root break away. Some growers use two misters per plant in case one fails.

Because plants grow a large delicate root system the marijuana plants are difficult to move or rearrange once they are established in a spot. This can decrease yields if there are bare spots in the growing area.

Aeroponics, like the NFT system described below, seems to be from the sci-fi school of gardening. It is said they are how horticulture will be practiced in the future. Let's hope a long time in the future. Though the systems can be made to work, there is little evidence that they offer any big advantage for the high level of maintenance they require.

Nutrient Film (NFT)

The nutrient film technique waters plants from the bottom with nutrient solution pumped from a reservoir. The nutrient-rich water flows down narrow gutter or grow tubes on which the marijuana plants are placed. Often capillary mats are laid along the bottom of the grow tubes. The mats are made of urethane, which holds some water and helps saturate the medium holding the plants. Kits are available for NFT systems, but homemade systems using plastic gutters are relatively easy to set up. Water is sent to the gutter through 1/2 inch plastic pipe. A small plastic faucet-like device makes it possible to adjust the flow of water along the gutter. Excess water is returned to the reservoir through more 1/2 inch pipe. Several gutters or grow tubes can be connected to a water re-circulating system.

Many kinds of growing media can be used with NFT systems as long as they have some water-wicking properties. Because the water is delivered from the bottom, the medium has to be capable of drawing the nutrient solution up towards the plants' roots, especially when the marijuana is young and the roots are not fully developed. Rockwool, for example, works well because it soaks up water like a sponge. Volcanic rock or ceramic beads should be mixed with about 25% medium sized vermiculite for water absorption. Soil-based media should be cut with similar amounts of vermiculite.

NFT systems also require a special kind of container. The bottom of the container has to be open so that the growing media can absorb the water as it flows along the bottom of the gutter or grow tube. Hard plastic containers for NFT systems have screens on the bottom. Also popular are plastic grow bags. Bags are easy to shape to the gutter, so that the medium can absorb the maximum amount of the water flowing by. Grow bags with small holes along the bottom are made for NFT systems, although you can fabricate your own.

Bottom watering is the weak part of this system. NFT systems work well once the plants are established, and their roots extend down to the water. Before that, the growing medium has to draw up enough water to hydrate the plant's young roots. Squat containers filled less than 6 inches above the water flow work ok. Even so, a little hand watering might be needed to quickly establish small marijuana plants.

NFT systems are fairly dependable in operation; it's just that both the ebb & flow and drip systems are much easier to set up and do a better job of growing.

Chapter 2   Scoping Out Equipment

Getting the right equipment is important in setting up a hydro unit. Since marijuana is being grown, the system has to be as fail-safe as possible. Smart growers set up systems designed to both to avoid accidents, and minimize the consequences should one occur. Ease in taking a system apart is also a prime consideration. In this chapter we will look at the hardware of hydro, and easy ways to get the right stuff.

At one time it was easier to buy complete, ready-made hydro systems because the individual parts needed to set up a system were hard to find. This is no longer the case, at least for drip or ebb-&-flow systems. Besides being a lot less expensive to set up your own system, grower-designed systems can be more easily adapted to the space available than ready-made systems. We will burn the next three chapters looking at the parts needed to set up a working grow.

Tables

Tables are used to raise the growing trays above the reservoir. This is so the nutrient solution can be returned to the reservoir by gravity at the end of a watering cycle.

The size of the table used is determined by the size of the system desired, and the tray sizes available. A 1000-watt light system set for maximum 'sea of green' production will fit into a 4-foot wide space. The growing area can be 6 to 8-feet long. The grower needs two 4-foot square trays, or one 4-foot square and one 2x4-foot tray. Smaller systems with 400 or 600-watt lights will use a single 4-foot tray.

The tables can be bought, or fashioned out of plywood and 2x4 inch lumber. Banquet tables are inexpensive, come in many sizes, and are sturdy. A sturdy table is necessary because water is heavy. When looking for tables remember that the tray has to be a few inches wider than the table, so that the plastic pipe connecting the tray to the reservoir can be easily installed.

Trays and Grow Tubes

Plastic trays with high sides make it easy to set up either ebb & flow or drip hydro systems. The trays hold the plants in the medium chosen for growing, such as rockwool cubes, or containers holding a growing medium. In the ebb & flow system the tray is flooded with nutrient solution at periodic intervals (see chapter 6). The drip system waters plants through small gauge tubing (spaghetti line), and works well when containers are used.

The trays come in various sizes, like 2x4 foot up to 4x8 foot. The 2x4 foot or 4 foot square trays are available at most indoor grow shops. Large trays, like 4x8 foot are some- what harder to set up. They need a large reservoir (100 gallons), for example. You may have to use shims on the side of tray furthest away from the pump so the nutrient solution properly drains back into the reservoir at the end of the watering cycle. Proper filling and draining should be considered when purchasing any tray. The tray should be easy to keep level at all corners so that no standing water remains in the trays between watering cycles.

The high sides on most trays minimize the potential of flooding should a malfunction occur. The trays can also be fitted with an overflow valve, a small pipe of 1 inch or more, used to re-circulate nutrient solution back to the reservoir should it rise above a specified level in the tray. Overflow valves are a must where reservoir capacity exceeds the water holding capacity of the tray.

Another kind of tray is the grow tube, usually a 6 inch (15.24 cm) diameter plastic pipe, with holes cut in it at various intervals for plant containers. Half-inch pipe is used to water the plants and to return unused nutrient solution to the reservoir. Grow tubes are often used with aeroponics, where nutrient solution is misted onto the roots of the plant, and NFT systems (nutrient film). Because of the use of specialized parts, kits are the best option for setting up one of these systems.

Hydro systems using grow tubes or plastic gutters are by nature more complex because they have more parts. They are more difficult to disassemble for cleaning, for example. When growing, the marijuana is at set spacing in grow tubes. This makes it harder to move the plants to take the best advantage of available light.

RESERVOIRS

Reservoirs need not be special equipment. Heavy-duty plastic storage containers, or plastic garbage cans of about 30 gallons are ideal for most situations. Which one is used is determined by the height of the table on which the trays are placed. Storage containers are usually lower to the ground, and work well when the grow room has a low ceiling (7-8 feet).

Larger hydroponic reservoirs are available, some 150 gallons or more. Larger reservoirs have both advantages and disadvantages. You can mix large amounts of nutrient solution at one time in a large reservoir, for example, which can be an advantage.

Potential disadvantages come into play when you consider the water holding capacity of the trays used. A 4x4 foot tray with 8-inch sides holds about 30 gallons of water. If a reservoir of 30 gallons is used, even if the system malfunctions, and the pumps don't shut off, the tray will not overflow. I should emphasize that this is not a common occurrence, since the timing units that control the pump are very dependable. Nonetheless, marijuana cultivators always need to look at what may happen if a part does not operate properly. Using reservoirs and trays that hold about the same amount of water minimizes the consequences should the system malfunction.

Reservoir water in the growing area does not usually r equire heating, if the space is kept in the optimal temperature range, 60°F nights and 85°F during the lighting cycle. During colder months, insulating reservoirs from cold floors with a rug or other materials is usually sufficient. In extremely cold temperatures, a water heater made for aquariums might be helpful.

Some growers aerate the water in reservoirs with aquarium aerators. Though this adds oxygen to the water, so does pumping the water out into the trays. In most cases aerators are not needed.

Pumps used for hydroponic units have greatly improved with the introduction of small-capacity submersible pumps. These pumps are rated to move 10 to 15 gallons of water per minute (GPM). In most cases the actual flow is less because the water is pumped uphill to the trays. These pumps are very reliable in that they don't clog easily and can be used without a filter. Properly prepared organic nutrient solutions can also be used with these units if the solution is filtered. One of these pumps can easily supply a 4x4 foot tray in an ebb & flow system, or up to 25 lines in a drip system.

Higher capacity pumps are easily available but growers should consider that the capacity of the pump should be matched to the system used. A 50 gallon per minute pump, for example, will have much more of a kick when it turns on than the 10 to 15 gallon one. This 50 gpm pump will deliver water to 100 plants or more. They also work well when water has to be moved some distance uphill (8 feet or more). In smaller systems, high capacity pumps can cause problems such as the force (kickback) when the water is turned on.

When using bigger pumps the pipe used to deliver the water needs to be tied down, and the tubing directed so that it does not spray or splash over the sides of the tray. The pressure with which the nutrient solution is delivered decreases as the amount of tubing and number of plants increases. Growers need to balance these factors with the size of the pump chosen.

Often, ready-made systems have larger pumps than are called for, and are fitted with filters, which tend to slow down the pump flow. These filters can cut off the flow of water if they clog up, and require frequent cleaning. Like smaller reservoirs, smaller pumps are a much better solution in many situations. The smaller pumps don't require filters and come with a lead, which easily snaps into the 1/2-inch plastic pipe typically used by hydro enthusiasts.

Higher velocity pumps are used in certain hydro systems, such as aeroponics. This is to force the nutrient solution through the small emitters used with these systems, and lessen the chance of the system clogging.

Larger systems for growing marijuana can be made using several of these relatively fail-safe smaller pumps rather than one high velocity unit. Growers should consider their needs in terms of a "balanced" hydro system rather than a high power one. Matching equipment to how it is actually going to be used is imperative in setting up a reliable automated system.

Since these pumps are submersed in the reservoir they should be plugged into a circuit with a **ground fault circuit interrupter,** which will shut off the electricity if there is a problem. The pumps should also be shut off when the reservoir is being serviced or filled.

Outdoor marijuana cultivators also sometimes use pumps to move water. Solar powered pumps are available. See chapter 9 on outdoor growing for more info.

TIMERS

Controlling the pump is the timer, which activates the pump for a set amount of time at regular intervals. Hydro growing became a lot more reliable with the recent

introduction of low-cost (about $30) digital timers. These timers turn the pump on and off with an electronic switch, rather than mechanically, like older models.

With these digital timers, growers have much more control over the watering cycle of plants. These grounded timers typically can be programmed for up to 12 cycles per day. Cycle time can be programmed for from 1 minute to 24 hours per cycle. Three short watering cycles of 4 minutes or less per day are often used on 4 foot indoor plants, for example. More watering cycles can be added if the plants get bigger. Similarly, less water is used on smaller plants.

Mechanical timer suitable for controlling lights.

Digital timers should be considered a must for hydro marijuana growers. The timers have a capacity of 15 amps and will run many pumps. These timers are very reliable, and many have battery back-up in case of power failure. The timers have made successful hydro growing much easier. Most failures occur from growers turning off a system for servicing, and forgetting to turn it back on.

Digital timers can also be used to control a 1000-watt H.I.D. light, but the less-expensive, grounded mechanical timers will work just as well for electric lights. The lights only need to be switched on and off once a day during flowering. During vegetative growth the grow lights may run continuously.

Higher capacity timers that will control several H.I.D. lights are available. These timers need to be wired into the electrical system by a competent electrician. The timers should be grounded for safe operation. For extra safety they should be wired into a ground fault circuit interrupter (see below).

Ground Fault Circuit Interrupter

Mentioned many times already is the ground fault circuit interrupter (GFCI), used to prevent shock where water and electricity can come into contact. GFCI units should be considered a must for hydro growers. All pumps, timers, and lights should be run through a ground fault circuit interrupter.

Ground fault circuit interrupters are inexpensive and are easily wired into the space of any regular grounded wall electric outlet.

Plastic Pipe

Plastic pipe is used to transport the nutrient solution from the reservoir to the marijuana plants. Most hydro systems use standard snap-together 1/2 inch pipe. "T" or "L" connectors are used to divide the pipe, or change the direction the pipe is going. The ends of the pipe are capped off with a special plastic pressure fitting in some hydro systems, such as drip or aeroponics. The 1/2 inch plastic pipe is also be used for draining the systems and returning water to the reservoir.

Drip systems use small gauge plastic tubing, called spaghetti line, to deliver water from the 1/2 inch line to each individual plant. A small tool is used to puncture a hole in the 1/2 inch pipe. This pipe is fitted with a small plastic part to which the spaghetti line is attached.

Fans

Fans are used to move air in the growing area, and also to bring fresh air into the grow. Fans help to control several growing conditions necessary to maintain optimum growth. They help keep the temperature in the growing area within acceptable parameters (under 90F.), for example. They also help replenish the carbon dioxide in the air, which plants use to grow.

Fans also help inhibit plant diseases such as molding, to which marijuana is susceptible. Insects also have a harder time becoming established in a well-ventilated space.

A single fan is usually sufficient for a small space. Larger fans, run at low speeds, make less noise than smaller fans, which need higher speeds to move the same amount of air. Fans equipped with a thermostat can be helpful. You can also program fans to be on throughout the light cycle. Air movement should be directed over the marijuana plants. A slow breeze on plants is very beneficial.

Larger growing systems with several lights may need more than one fan. One would be used to bring fresh air into the growing area, and the other to direct air movement around the plants.

Plant Supports

New varieties of marijuana are often top-heavy late in the flowering cycle. The plants require support for optimum production. As an additional consideration, unsupported plants spend time and energy producing a woody, thick, stalk to support this weight, at the expense of flower production.

Plant supports made with plastic fencing. Photo: Sam Pedro

Simple supports such as bamboo sticks are sometimes used. These supports can work OK if there is enough growing medium to support the bamboo. However, bamboo can also be quite dangerous to work around, if these plant supports are at eye level. The ends of the bamboo branch should be fitted with rubber tips for eye protection. You can also wear glasses when working around marijuana with these kinds of supports.

A better support system is a grid of plastic or light metal fencing hung 2-3 feet above the bed of the growing tray.

The marijuana grows up through the grid and leans on the fencing for support. The supports are hung at about 3/4 the final height of the marijuana. Plants that finish at 4 feet, for example, should have the support grid hung at 3 feet.

Negative Ion Generators

Air movement, which is necessary for plant growth, unfortunately spreads the distinct smell of growing marijuana. The smell is caused as the small THC glands break off the marijuana and the oil within is released into the air. With or without fans some smell is inevitable.

Ion generators electrostatically remove smell from the air by attracting microscopic particulates such as those that cause the sweet scent of marijuana.

Ion generators vary in capacity from small room size units to generators made for industrial use. Get the most powerful unit you can afford. A small ion generator may not remove all of the smell emanating from the growing space.

Temperature/Humidity Gauge

A gauge that reads both temperature and humidity will set you back less than ten bucks, and is well worth it for the information it supplies. Marijuana grows best in temperatures of 75° to 90°F during the light cycle, for example. Humidity of less than 70% is also optimal, especially when the marijuana is late in the flowering stage.

Without a gauge it is difficult to adjust equipment such as fans, or heaters if they are needed. What you don't know can hurt you.

Equipment that turns on ventilation when either the temperature or humidity exceeds programmed levels is available.

Mylar or Reflective material

You're going to be paying for electricity to run your lights, so you want to get as much as possible to the plants. Surrounding the growing area with reflective material keeps the light where it belongs, on the plants.

Mylar with a mirror finish is the best material for this. Other material such as white paint, or aluminum foil will also work.

High Tech Equipment

Movable mylar shade reflects light back to plants.

Once growers establish a grow, they often upgrade the system they are using, in order to be more productive and less detectable. The object is often to set up what is known as a 'closed system'. The closed system uses pumped in carbon dioxide, CO_2, usually from a tank, and an air conditioner or heater to control temperatures. In a closed system the grower feeds the marijuana high amounts CO_2 to enhance the growth of the plants.

In low tech systems fresh air is brought in to replenish the CO_2 in the air because without CO_2 plants will not grow. In the 'closed system' the CO_2 is supplied by the grower and the air conditioner is used to keep the air at optimum temperature, 82° F. This keeps the CO_2 in the growing area where the marijuana thrives on it. It also minimizes venting to the outside where the smell of growing marijuana can cause detection problems.

Other high tech equipment might include sensors to detect high temperatures and humidity, or video equipment that lets you view the grow from a remote location.

Curiously, computer programs for growing marijuana or most other plants is not available. Such systems are feasible, but would be very expensive at present. They may also have limited applications - the fact is that growing great marijuana still requires a lot of hand work. If you consider that equipment like digital timers contain computer-like chips, growers are already using computer technology, even if it is not run from a central program.

Carbon Dioxide

Carbon Dioxide, (CO_2), is a gas, which is contained in small amounts in the air around us. CO_2 is essential in the growth process of plants. Marijuana is no exception: the plant has small openings under its leaves that separates CO_2 from the air and draws it into the plant. The 350 parts per million (ppm) in the air is enough to grow marijuana if the air in the growing area is vented to bring in a lot of fresh air.

Marijuana growers often supply CO_2 directly to plants for two reasons. High concentrations of CO_2 makes marijuana grow and flower much faster. With CO_2 and an air conditioner, a "closed system" can also be set up. Air does need to be vented out of the grow, and the CO_2 is held in, keeping the marijuana purring along in overdrive.

Marijuana can grow twice as fast as normal in high amounts of CO_2, and will flower up to a couple of weeks faster. Under CO_2 enrichment the marijuana will grow optimally in higher temperatures, 85° F instead of 80° F.

Carbon dioxide is produced by burning hydrocarbons. Cars, for example, produce huge amounts of CO_2. Marijuana growers usually use CO_2 from tanks, although a few use CO_2 derived directly from burning natural gas or propane. A pilot light like that on a stove or water heater, for example, is enough to double the normal amount of CO_2 in a small growing area. Burning hydrocarbons for CO_2 production has limited applications however, because it adds both heat and humidity to the growing area. A cold growing room or greenhouse where the heat is beneficial could use CO_2 produced by burning. Again, humidity is the limiting factor. It is seldom possible to increase CO_2 levels beyond twice normal, 700ppm, using natural gas or propane, without increasing humidity beyond acceptable levels. CO_2 generators made for horticulture minimize the heat and humidity produced by burning, and have a high CO_2 output. They are available at many hydro stores.

In the 'closed system' the CO_2 is supplied by the grower and the air conditioner is used to keep the air at optimum temperature, 82°F.

CO_2 in pressurized tanks make it very easy to supply 2 to 3 times the normal amounts of CO_2 to the growing area. The CO_2 is released from the tank with a regulator available at hydro stores. The CO_2 is then blown around the grow room with a fan. Marijuana uses CO_2 only when the lights are on, so a timer is used to synchronize the release of CO_2 with the light cycle. Marijuana can use up to 1200 ppm of CO_2 in the air of the grow room. Tests that measure CO_2 levels are available for about $10 a hit. Electronic measuring units run about $500, and let you measure CO_2 levels anytime.

Regulators, which are screwed on to the CO_2 tank, are pretty simple. They usually release from 1/2 to 2 cubic feet of CO_2 per hour. Most growers release a constant set amount of CO_2 throughout the light-cycle. Growers not using a "closed system" time releases of CO_2 to the shutting down of vents to the outside. Timers that accomplish this are available at grow shops. That way the gas stays longer in the grow, where it is eagerly taken in by the marijuana.

With an air conditioner to cool the grow room sufficiently ventilation to the outside is seldom needed. The carbon dioxide stays in the growing area until used by the marijuana.

Air Conditioner

Heat is a limiting factor in many grow rooms, especially those with multiple lights. Marijuana essentially stops growing in temperatures above 90° F. Low tech systems vent air to the outside to cool the growing area, and also bring in fresh air, that contains CO_2, which the marijuana needs to grow. Unfortunately, venting air to the outside can be a source of problems for the grower, such as detection, and loss of CO_2-enriched air. Due to the aromatic quality of marijuana out door venting is risky. Growers often spend considerable amounts of money on equipment made to cover the smell of growing marijuana. Venting also makes it harder to apply CO_2, which dramatically increases growth rates.

The solution is often an air conditioner. Air conditioning does many positive things such as, running the growing area at optimum temperatures, or allowing very efficient CO_2 enrichment. If CO_2 enrichment is used, air conditioning makes it unnecessary to vent air to the outside. Air conditioners also take some of the humidity out of the air of the grow room. Growing marijuana processes lots of water, which it takes in through its roots and releases through its leaves. High humidity also necessitates ventilation to the outside in low tech set-ups.

Growers should get as large an air conditioner as possible, especially if they might add lights to the growing area in the future. Models with high cooling capacity cost only a little more to buy, and about the same to run. The AC is run on the re-circulate mode, and the heat the unit produces is vented out of the growing area. In addition, air conditioners drip water which can be directed out of the growing area, or collected and piped to the water of a reservoir for use by the plants.

The air conditioner is set to maintain the grow room air at 80°-85° F during the light cycle. Growers usually shut off air conditioning during darkness, although growers might run the AC for a couple of hours after the lights shut off in hot weather, or to remove humidity from the grow room.

Dehumidifier

Dehumidifiers are useful in grow spaces located in cold, wet climates. Besides removing humidity from the air, they also add heat to the space. Heat may be needed during cold winter months, at least during night cycles when the lights are off. Keeping night temperatures above 60° F is optimum. Humidity levels below 70% will mitigate the possibilities of some plant diseases like mold or mildew. These machines are fairly expensive to buy and operate, but they can save a crop during adverse outside weather conditions.

The dehumidifiers are easy to use, just set the machine to remove the desired amount of humidity from the air, or to add heat if it is needed. The unit has to be emptied periodically of the water, which it collects. Often the water is pumped to a reservoir for use by plants.

One other use for dehumidifiers is during the drying of large amounts of marijuana. Drying marijuana fairly quickly is best for preserving potency and taste. Low humidity levels of about 40% and temperatures above 70° F are best for drying pot.

Sensors

Techie type growers can equip growing spaces with the latest in James-Bond-like technology. Remote video cameras, or sensors that will contact the grower in emergencies such as busts, break-ins, fire, or flooding are available. Check out home automation sites on the web to locate this type of equipment. Much of this equipment can be installed with very little wiring, and is, as might be expected, pricey. Keep in mind also that plug-in equipment will not operate during power outages.

Power Washer

Intensive cultivation by growing the same crop over and over in the same space requires cleanliness. Keeping grit and grime out of the growing area is of prime importance to a successful grow. The reservoirs and trays used by hydro growers, for example, should be cleaned between crops. Deep cleaning of grow room equipment might be done twice a year if the grow is running well. A power washer can keep this chore from becoming a drag.

Power washers are cheap and make quick work of sizable cleaning jobs. Don't try cleaning in the growing area with a power washer. Equipment should be cleaned away from electrical equipment.

Chapter 3

LIGHTING SYSTEMS, REFLECTORS and LIGHT MOVERS

Marijuana needs light for photosynthesis, the process by which it grows. Indoor marijuana cultivators use electric lights as the light source, rather than the sun, to grow plants. Three kinds of lights are commonly used to grow marijuana: the two types of high intensity discharge lights (HID), (metal halide and high-pressure sodium lamps), and fluorescent lights.

Fluorescent Lights

The common fluorescent light can be used to grow marijuana both during the cutting (clone) stage, and until flowering. They are used less often for flowering even though newer versions of the fluorescent shop lights work as well as metal halides for this purpose.

The basic fluorescent light is the 4-foot shop light, which comes with a reflector, and should be ready to plug into a grounded outlet. A 2-bulb unit can be purchased for less than ten dollars. Fluorescent lights are available in other configurations, but most of these have not yet been improved by electronic technology.

The big improvement in the 4-foot shop light has been the substitution of an electronically controlled ballast weighing a few ounces, for one that weighs 3-4 pounds. The ballast controls the voltage to the bulb where various gases are activated to produce light. The electronic ballasts also make the lights more efficient so they draw 15% less current than older models. Watt per watt this means these lights produce nearly as much light as metal halide bulbs.

Make sure you are getting shop lights with these electronic

ballasts, it should be noted on the packaging. Each fourfoot, 2 light unit should weigh only a few pounds. Avoid units that require assembly - the shop light should be ready to plug in.

The low weight of each shop light makes it much easier to gang several units together for a low cost flowering light. Four shop lights weigh only about 12 pounds, including the electronic ballasts. For optimum results these lights are kept within 3-4 inches of growing marijuana plants. For this reason the shop lights are most often set up so

Fluorescent Starter System

that they can be easily raised or lowered to conform to the plants' needs.

Some growers use stationary lights where the marijuana plants will not be growing quickly, like during cloning. In a growing space with low ceilings (4-5 feet), the shop lights can also be installed so that they are stationary. Some growers cover both the ceiling and walls of the growing space with the fluorescent shop lights.

The low cost "cool" white fluorescent bulb works as well as most others for growing marijuana. The bulb produces a lot of light in the blue spectrum, and is one of the highest in total light output, about 3200 lumens per 40-watt tube. Blue light stimulates the rooting of cuttings and the healthy vegetative growth of marijuana. Pruned marijuana plants up to 3 feet high at harvest can be grown with fluorescent lights. Larger plants may not form quality buds on their lower branches.

For the flowering of marijuana "warm" white fluorescent tubes are slightly better than cool white tubes. Increases in the weight of flowers of up to 5% have been noted with the use of with warm white tubes, but they cost a lot more.

For cloning, bulbs producing light largely in the blue spectrum is best, so cool white bulbs work well. The gourmet bulb for cuttings is the pricey GE Chroma 50®, a photography light.

High Pressure Sodium Light

The most popular and versatile grow light is the high-pressure sodium light (HPS), which was developed for street lighting. These bulbs produce about 35% more light than fluorescent and metal halide lights, for the same amount of electricity. Much of this light is in the far-red spectrum, which stimulates flowering, but the lights also emit almost as much blue spectrum light as the halide.

High-pressure sodium lights put out substantially more

overall light (50,000 lumens for a 400-watt HPS, compared to 35,000 for the Halide. Because HPS bulbs have a much longer life, most growers prefer these lights. Growers who are going to include only one H.I.D. light in their system should consider a high-pressure sodium lamp.

Vertical & Horizontally Mounted HPS lights.

High-pressure sodium lights come in many sizes, from small 125-watt lamps to 1000-watt lights. Lights made specifically for growing are preferred because they come with reflecting hoods. HPS grow lights also come in 250, 400, and 600-watt models.

All lamps include heavy ballasts. The ballast is sometimes mounted into the hood and light reflector, especially in lower watt models. Because of the weight of the ballast, external ballasts, connected to the light by a power cord, are preferred. The external ballasts are easy to position so that they cannot come into contact with water.

Lights and ballasts also have to be matched, both for wattage and other manufacturer specifications. Some brands of HPS bulbs may not work with all HPS ballasts. Also, high-pressure sodium and metal halide ballasts are not interchangeable. However, one company has developed a ballast that can work with both halide and HPS bulbs.

High-pressure sodium lights are mounted in their reflectors either vertically or horizontally. Most vertically mounted lights are high wattage models, typically a 1000-watt HPS. Though considered by some to be the "old model," vertically mounted lights can work as well or better than the more common horizontally mounted HPS lights. Vertically mounted lights work well when equipped with a large parabolic reflector. The large reflector makes the use of a light mover unnecessary.

The smaller 125 and 250-watt HPS units are effective for small growing areas. The 250-watt unit covers a space of about 2x3 feet. Attempting to enlarge the space by raising the light does little to increase yield, since yield is dependent on the intensity of light the plants receive. Both HPS and metal halide lights are hot and must be kept a minimum of 18 inches from plants.

Metal Halide Lights

Sodium bulbs also maintain their lumen output for a much longer time, so the bulbs are usable for about 50% longer than metal halide.

These lights moved indoor marijuana cultivation into a new era, the era of high intensity discharge (HID) lighting. When introduced as a grow light in the mid 1970s they were far easier to use than the fluorescent units then available. Halide lights produce light high in the blue spectrum, which is used by plants during vegetative growth. The lights come in sizes similar to those of the high-pressure sodium lights.

Because halides are somewhat higher in blue spectrum light some growers prefer them to high-pressure sodium lights, especially during vegetative growth. But because the total light output of the HPS is so much higher the difference is negligible. Sodium bulbs also maintain their lumen output for a much longer time, so the bulbs are usable for about 50% longer than metal halide.

Halide lights put out light at about the same intensity as fluorescent lights equipped with electronic ballasts, per watt of electricity used. Cool white fluorescents produce light of a similar spectrum to that of the halide. Because these new fluorescent units are lightweight, some of the advantages the halide had over fluorescent light have vanished.

A set-up with five, 2 bulb, 4-foot fluorescent shop lights, has about the same light output as a 400-watt metal halide. Price conscious growers who want to set up a personal low cost system can find the fluorescents in any "big box" hardware store for about 1/3 the price of halides.

Halide bulbs are more delicate than the high-pressure sodium bulbs. A few growers have reported the bulbs cracking while the lights are in operation. Always turn off H.I.D lights when spraying any liquids in the growing area. Like HPS lights, halides are hot and should be kept a minimum of 18 inches away from plants.

Plugging In

Once you choose a light you need to plug it in safely. As mentioned previously, a *ground fault circuit interrupter*, installed in place of a regular-grounded electric outlet, is strongly recommended. Power strips, with several plugs, are also available with this feature.

For safe operation, H.I.D. lights should be turned on and off with a timer. The ballast is the most dangerous part of both high-pressure sodium and metal halide lights. This is especially true when the lights are turned on, and a surge of current is drawn through the ballast. Ballasts should also be located in a dry part of the growing area, and positioned so that water cannot get near them. Never spray liquids in the growing area while the grow lights are on; this could cause the bulbs to crack.

Light Movers

Light movers are used to move a H.I.D. light in a set pattern over the plants. Most often movers are used with high wattage 1000-watt lights. Various designs are available.

A light mover that moves a single light back and forth over the plants is used most often. More complex models moving several lights in a circular fashion are also available.

The 1000-watt lights are put on a light mover to extend the amount of growing space a horizontally mounted light can cover. Plants need to be kept at least 18 inches away from a stationary 1000-watt high-pressure sodium bulb; otherwise they will slowly cook. Moving the light mitigates this potential overheating problem somewhat. But growers can also hang lights so they are slightly further away from plants, 2 feet, instead of using a mover.

Horizontally mounted high-pressure sodium lights on light movers

On a light mover, a 1000-watt HPS can cover about a 4x8 foot space. Without a mover, the light will only cover a space about 4x6 foot, when hung the same distance from the plants. Remember, a larger space does not necessarily guarantee a larger harvest. The smaller system may yield as much as the larger one, because of the more intense concentration of light.

The systems that move a single light are known to be reliable, but growers should still consider whether they want a hot 1000-watt light to be moving. Over time, the wiring that moves with the lights on a mover is more prone to fraying or breaking, than wiring on a stationary light. Setting up a fail-safe system is of prime consideration.

Light movers are usually not used for lights other than the 1000-watt high intensity discharge bulbs. Even with the 1000 watt lights, a light mover is not always necessary. The vertically mounted 1000-watt HPS with a large parabolic reflector, for example, is not usually hung on a light mover.

Reflectors

Reflectors are made to keep light pointing towards the marijuana plants. For example, half of the light from a horizontal grow light is emitted upwards away from the plants. The reflector bounces the light back towards the plants.

A lot of usable light is lost through poor reflectors, but fortunately getting a good reflector is easy. The main consideration is that the grow light mounting holds the bulb so that it is in the center of the reflector. This keeps the light that is reflected towards the plants evenly distributed. A good reflector helps avoid hot spots and low producing sections in the growing area.

Reflectors come in many forms, from small, box-like reflectors to the 4 foot diameter parabolic reflectors that make the grow room look like it's been invaded by space aliens. Reflectors are usually included when a light is purchased, and can also be purchased separately.

One other reflector system should be mentioned. These reflectors are designed to remove heat from the growing area. The reflectors are equipped with a glass covering, a vent, and a small fan to move heat away from the lights and out of the growing area. Several lights can be connected to one system. These systems cut the amount of light plants receive by up to 10%, but can be useful if the growing area often overheats, over 90° F.

Clonig system using rockwool cubes

Chapter 4

WATER, NUTRIENTS, & GROWING MEDIA

"Feed them and they will grow", is how one grower summed up marijuana cultivation. She was correct; nutrients are an integral part of successful cultivation.

In hydro growing, the media themselves often do not have much nutrient in them. The cultivator supplies the fertilizer to the plants, sometimes by adding it to the medium, but most often by mixing it with the water. This way, marijuana is fertilized every time it is watered. The plants are never without adequate food and respond in kind.

Indoor marijuana growing has become a science, since hydro cultivators now understand exactly what it takes to grow great stuff. With a couple pieces of inexpensive equipment growers can easily monitor the nutrient solution and adjust it to optimize fertilizer levels.

The **total dissolved solids** (TDS) meter, reads the total strength of the fertilizer that is added to the water reservoir in parts per million (ppm). This small piece of electronic equipment has made successful hydro growing on a small scale possible. Growers no longer have to wonder if they are feeding their plants too much or too little food.

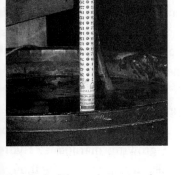

Dissolved solids wand measures the strength of the nutrient solution

The other piece of equipment essential to hydro growing is the **pH monitor**. This device measures the acidity or alkalinity of the nutrient solution. A pH of 7 is neutral, while lower pH numbers are acid, and higher numbers alkaline. Big deal, you might say, what difference does pH make? More than you might expect! Marijuana will grow in a relatively large pH range, but will thrive in a much more narrow range. On the fourteen-point scale, marijuana thrives in a slightly acidic (6.5) environment around its roots.

The pH of the nutrient solution also affects the uptake o
nutrients. Nutrient solutions with pH levels that are wa
out of whack can lock up nutrients making them unavail
able to the plant. Growing problems are often pH related
When you consider that the water, the fertilizer blend
and the growing media all affect the pH, you can see tha
a pH monitor is more than handy.

Rockwool, for example, a popular hydro growing media
has a very alkaline pH. To counter this, growers conditio
the rockwool by soaking it in an acid bath, pH 5, befor
use. The nutrient solution is also kept in the acid, 5.8 pH
range to counter the alkaline pH of the rockwool. Doin
this without a pH monitor would be difficult.

Older style pH test kits use reactive paper strips, whic
turn different colors at various pH readings. They are fairl
accurate. The kits include a set number of tests, usuall
10, and will work when only a small number of tests wi
be done. An outdoor grower, for example, may need just
few tests to determine the conditioning needed for an ou
door grow. Indoor growers, who need to monitor the p
of the medium and watering solution on a continuous ba
sis, could use reactive paper if the pH meter fails, but wi
also need to have a pH meter.

Electronic meters measuring the fertilizer levels (dissolve
solids meter) and pH of the nutrient solution take a lo
of the guesswork out of growing marijuana. Hydr
growing without them is like trying to drive without
speedometer. You might get away with it for a while, bu
you'll never really know how fast you're going.

Nutrients

Mineral nutrients and a few gases are the food marijuan
uses to grow. For the most part plant food is taken up throug
the root system and is transported throughout the plant
Good nutrition is essential for lush, healthy plants.

Nutrient solutions fit into the big picture of marijuana cultivation as an essential part of the intriguing way in which plants grow. Marijuana uses light to drive the oxidation of the mineral nutrients, the slow burn of plant life. The plant uses light and the nutrients to manufacture chlorophyll, which gives the marijuana plant its deep green color. The water in the solution keeps the plant tissue turgid and upright.

One other essential in the growth of plants is the accumulation of carbon, a major constituent of plant tissue. Plants derive carbon from the carbon dioxide in the air around its leaves. I mention these processes not to confuse, but to summarize what growers can "feed" the marijuana in a controllable way.

Fertilizer mixes containing all the mineral nutrients essential for growing marijuana are easy to find at hydro stores. Most of these mixes are of high quality, but expensive. National brands, like Miracle Grow®, Peters®, and Plant Marvel® dissolve easily, and have some formulas which contain most of the essential nutrients (see next section).

What's in fertilizer mixes is no mystery. A typical mix is made up mostly (90%) of three elemental fertilizers. These are nitrogen, phosphorus, and potassium.

What's in fertilizer mixes is no mystery. A typical mix is made up mostly (90%) of three elemental fertilizers. These are nitrogen, phosphorus, and potassium. Three other essential nutrients, calcium, magnesium and sulfur may make up 5-8% of a complete fertilizer blend. Several other micro-nutrients are essential for hydro growing, but make up less than 2% of the fertilizer mix.

Fertilizer strength is listed by how much nitrogen, phosphorous and potassium a mix contains. This is called the NPK. A 15-30-15 NPK fertilizer contains 15% nitrogen, 30% phosphorus, and 15% potassium (K). A 30-30-15 fertilizer has twice the nitrogen of the first listing.

Fertilizer mixes should include all the nutrients listed on the following chart except oxygen, carbon dioxide, and light. The fertilizer is mixed with water as the reservoir is filled. Hydro fertilizers should dissolve easily in water, since the plants can only use dissolved nutrients. Many ready-made hydro fertilizers are liquids. Crystalline and fine powder fertilizers also dissolve readily.

Marijuana grows well in the 800-1500 ppm nutrient range. Use the lower concentrations on small plants. Lower concentrations of fertilizer are also often used late in the flowering cycle. Marijuana will tolerate up to 2500 ppm of fertilizer for short periods but over time, high concentrations of nutrients will damage plants.

A 1/2 cup of strong fertilizer such as 30-30-15 will bring 30 gallons of water to a nutrient level of about 1000 ppm (parts per million), as measured with a dissolved solids meter. The reading drifts upward over a couple of hours and may reach 1200 ppm. Fertilizer blends with lower NPK readings will require more fertilizer to obtain the same 1000 ppm nutrient level. A lower level blend, such as 5-2-2 NPK, will require 2-3 cups to bring the same 30 gallons of nutrient solution to 1000 ppm nutrient level.

A good strategy for using ready-mixed fertilizers is to change brands if the marijuana has any problems growing. Different formulas have different amounts of micro- and macro-nutrients and may be more compatible with the water you are using. Even though micro-nutrients are used in very small amounts, a certain amount is essential for the well being of the plants. Deficiencies of minor nutrients can be hard to pinpoint.

The taste of marijuana flowers is often associated with the nutrients used for growing. Nutrients do affect the bouquet and flavor of the flowers. Very high nutrient levels late in the flowering stage are said to sometimes produce a chemical tasting harvest. The source of nitrogen in the fertilizer blend is also thought to affect the flavor. Calcium nitrate is the preferred source of nitrogen for many hydro growers. At the proper nutrient and pH levels most fertilizer blends will grow a good tasting crop.

Nutrient	Soluble	Source	pH	N-P-K
Nitrogen	++	Calcium Nitrate	al	15-0-0
	++	Potassium Nitrate	ac	15-0-45
	+	Ammonium Nitrate	ac	30-0-0
	+	Ammonium Phosphate	ac	10-30-0
	+	Fish Emulation or Meal	ac	5-2-2
	+	Blood Meal	ac	10-2-0
	+	Urea	ac	40-0-0
	-	Bat Guano	-	13-2-2
	-	Cottonseed Meal	ac	7-2-2
Phosphorous	-	Super Phosphate	ac	0-20-0
	++	Phosphoric Acid	ac	0-50-0
	-	Bone Meal	-	2-20-0
	+	Potassium Phosphate	ac	0-20-40
	+	Ammonium Phosphate	ac	10-40-0
	-	Bat Guano	-	0-4-1
Potassium	++	Muriate of Potash	-	0-0-50
	+	Potassium Sulfate	ac	0-0-45
	-	Greensand (micros)	-	0-2-5
Calcium	+	Hydrated Lime	al	
	+	Gypsum(calcium sulfate)		
	-	Dolomite		
Sulfur		Micro Nutrient Blend		
	+	Gypsum	-	
Magnesium	+	Magnesium Sulfate	-	
		(epsom salts)		
Iron	+	Iron Sulfate	ac	
	+	10% Iron Chelate	-	
		Micro Nutrient Blend		
Zinc		Micro Nutrient Blend		
Manganese		Micro Nutrient Blend		
Molybdenum		Micro Nutrient Blend		
Boron		Micro Nutrient Blend		
Micro Nutrients	-	pyrophillitic (pyro)clay kelp		
Oxygen		Air		
		Through The Roots		
Carbon Dioxide		Air Around Leaves		
		Gas		
		Hydrocarbon Burning		
Light		Sunlight		
		Electric Light		

A dissolved solids meter will give you a reading of the total amount of nutrients in the solution, not that of an individual nutrient. Growers choose what proportion of the major fertilizers they want using the NPK listing of the fertilizer.

Fertilizer blends with a high proportion of nitrogen fertilizer, such as 20-20-20 or 12-10-7 are often used during vegetative growth. Blends where the proportion of nitrogen is as high or higher than the amount of phosphorous are considered high nitrogen. Marijuana seems to like relatively high amounts of phosphate throughout its life cycle. During flowering, fertilizer blends higher in phosphates like 15-30-15 or 12-24-10 increase the flowering response of marijuana plants.

Over time, as the reservoir is filled and refilled, the nutrient solution becomes unbalanced. This is because the marijuana plants do not take in all the nutrients evenly; some are left behind and build up in the reservoir. Because of this, reservoirs are periodically cleaned and filled with new nutrient solution. How often the reservoirs should be recharged depends on a number of factors.

Some growers consistently go up to 2 months without flushing the reservoir. A balanced fertilizer blend is the key to having the marijuana draw in the nutrients relatively evenly. Potassium is one nutrient that sometimes builds up in reservoirs because some fertilizer formulas are very rich in it. In general, potassium levels should not be higher than either the nitrogen or phosphate level. An NPK like those above will all work, but 15-15-30 or 12-24-35 mixtures will lead to a build-up of potassium.

Another reason to clean out the reservoir is the particulate that accumulates there. Particulate is small pieces of roots, growing media, or un-dissolved fertilizer. Over time this will impede the flow of water through the system, or clog the tubes and drainage. Clean running systems using a balanced, well-dissolved nutrient solution will go the longest without flushing.

Understanding Nutrients

Mineral nutrients are the food of marijuana as we have seen. A quick look at each nutrient and how it affects plant growth will help growers optimize growth. It will also help in troubleshooting should problems arise.

NITROGEN is the primary nutrient in vegetative growth. It is responsible for the abundant growth and deep green color of marijuana. Plants deficient in nitrogen turn a paler green and the fan leaves turn yellow, beginning at the bottom of the plant. The leaf stems may turn purple. Too much nitrogen can burn plants. Plants that were growing very fast slow down and the leaves begin to curl as if the plant lacks water. Brown leaf tips may appear. The nitrate forms of nitrogen are the fastest acting. Other forms of nitrogen are converted to nitrate forms by bacteria before a plant can assimilate them. Nitrate nitrogen works noticeably better in cool weather.

PHOSPHORUS is associated with flower set. High phosphorus levels increase the size and number of flowers. Marijuana can use proportionately twice as much phosphorus as nitrogen during early flowering, and even more in the late flowering stage. Plants deficient in phosphorous are stunted, with the older leaves turning a dull green. Leaf stems turn reddish. Ripening of flowers may be delayed. Phosphorus levels don't often become toxic if the pH of the nutrient solution is correct. Excess phosphorus inhibits the uptake of other nutrients if the pH is out of whack.

POTASSIUM helps plants develop strong stems and a deep green color. Seed crops are also enhanced with sufficient amounts of potassium. For all that, seedless marijuana uses only about 1/2 the amount of potassium as phosphorus or nitrogen. Some nutrient formulas are excessively high in potassium, which will build up in reservoirs over time, and require flushing or cleaning the reservoir.

SULFUR is used by plants to regulate growth. Plants deficient in sulfur exhibit yellowing new leaves. Deficiencies are not common since sulfur-bearing rock is the source of many other plant nutrients. Plants need only about 1% sulfur in the nutrient mix, but marijuana will tolerate up to 5%. The higher levels may help inhibit some plant diseases, like molds and mildew.

CALCIUM is used in relatively high amounts by marijuana, and helps in root development and new growth. Up to 7% of some nutrient formulas may be calcium; other formulas may not contain this nutrient at all. Many municipal water supplies contain significant amounts of calcium. Hard water also contains this nutrient. Good growth requires only about 3% calcium, although the higher levels mentioned are seldom toxic.

MAGNESIUM aids plants in the manufacture of chlorophyll and new plant tissue. Marijuana needs only about 1% magnesium, but deficiencies can develop since the nutrient is left out of some fertilizer mixes. Yellowing older leaves, where only the veins remain green, is the first sign of deficiency.

IRON is used in small amounts, 1/2 of 1% of nutrient formulas. Yellow new growth, where the leaf veins remain green, indicates deficiency. This is not common if the nutrient formula contains iron. Iron is toxic in any but small amounts, and some iron supplements contain up to 10% iron. Bronzing of leaves is the symptom of overdose.

ZINC is another nutrient required in small amounts of less than 1% of nutrient blends. Distorted, curling of leaves is a sign of deficiency. Like iron, zinc is toxic in any but very small amounts.

MANGANESE and the following minerals are used in minuscule amounts by marijuana. They are easiest added to fertilizer blends in mixes including all or most minor nutrients. All can be toxic if overused. Yellow leaves at the top of the plant are a sign of manganese deficiency.

BORON sometimes becomes unavailable to plants when large amounts of calcium (7% or more) are used in the fertilizer blend. Symptoms include malformed flowers or new growth.

MOLYBDENUM deficiency is like that of nitrogen, yellowing of lower leaves.

COPPER is used in very small amounts. Copper is a pollutant in many water supplies. If you have copper pipes your plants will get enough of this mineral.

A few other nutrients like aluminum and chlorine are sometimes mentioned as essential to plants. Chlorine is present in all municipal water supplies. There is some disagreement if aluminum is actually needed. One other nutrient, silicon, is not essential, but is said to be helpful in promoting strong stems and healthy sap flow through marijuana plants.

pH

As discussed previously, the pH of the fertilizer solution affects how nutrients are absorbed by marijuana. Marijuana likes a slightly acidic, 6.5 pH for optimum growth. Some growing media, like rockwool, which is very alkaline, require a more acidic nutrient solution of pH 5.8. Nutrient solutions that are much too acidic or alkaline can render certain nutrients unavailable to the plant, even though they are in the fertilizer blend.

The pH of the nutrient solution is adjusted with products called **pH up** and **pH down**. These products contain highly concentrated forms of two chemicals. Phosphoric acid is used for pH down. Potassium, which is alkaline, is used for pH up. Thoroughly mix these products with the nutrient solution before the pH levels are read. A little goes a long way.

The pH can be affected by many factors such as the growing media, water, or the kind of fertilizer used to grow the marijuana plants. Many municipal water systems, for example, deliver water in the pH range of 8.0-8.3 because it preserves the piping system. Alkaline water like this could cause problems except for the fact that most fertilizer blends are quite acidic, which counteracts the water's alkaline pH. Calcium carbonate is the chemical often used by municipal systems to bring the water to this alkaline pH. As we have seen calcium is an essential nutrient in the cultivation of marijuana.

Water off the grid, such as that from wells or streams, may also contain high levels of nutrients like calcium (hard water). Usually water with nutrient levels of 200 ppm or less, as measured on the dissolved solids meter, will not cause problems. Growers will want an analysis of what's in water with mineral levels higher than 200 ppm. Whatever minerals are already in the water should not be in the fertilizer blend used.

The pH of the nutrient solution can also be adjusted by choosing your fertilizer carefully. Typically, nutrients are on the acid side of the pH scale. By mixing your own fertilizers you can adjust the mix so that little or no adjustments are needed. See the next section for details.

Mixing and Doctoring Fertilizer

Hydro growers have several options for obtaining fertilizers. There are many commercially blended complete hydroponic fertilizers available at indoor grow shops. Though they can be expensive, (sometimes very expensive), they are usually high quality and easy to mix. Most are complete and contain all the nutrients essential for plant growth. For growers with little knowledge of nutrients and plant growth, they are the easiest way to get started.

Once you get the hang of using fertilizers, growers can save considerable amounts of cash by mixing their own blends. For moderately priced hydro nutrients check out   http://www.hydroponicsales.com   or http://www.cropking.com on the net. Two other sites worth checking out are Mycotech and Bioworks, both of which sell botanical pest controls. These companies have listings of nursery supply houses that sell their products on their web sites. The supply companies also carry fertilizers. Most will sell retail at prices considerably less than are usually available at the neighborhood grow store.

The fertilizers sold at most hydro stores, for example, cost up to $10 per pound. Organic fertilizers can be even more expensive. If you are willing to mix together a few powders you can mix a top-notch fertilizer of your own for less than $1 per pound. You won't have to obtain each individual element, only those that are often left out of some fertilizer blends.

The nutrients most often left out of commercial fertilizer blends are calcium, magnesium, or sulfur. Professional straight growers often prefer to add these nutrients to the blend themselves because local water supplies may already contain some or all of these minerals. You can also match the pH of your fertilizer blend to local water conditions using various combinations of these three minerals. That way much less adjustment needs to be made to the pH of the nutrient solution.

Miracle Grow® blue (15-30-15), a national brand, is a complete formula except for two minerals, calcium and magnesium. A grower would need to add only 2 tablespoons of hydrated lime (for calcium) and 2 teaspoons of Epson Salts (for magnesium) per pound to make this into a usable complete, hydro fertilizer. Miracle Grow® also has a high nitrogen blend for tomatoes, which is good for vegetative growth. Use caution when blending: powdered fertilizer is acrid to the nose and eyes, and should be mixed in closed containers.

Peters Professional® fertilizers has several formulas both for flowering and vegetative growth. Many of these blends don't contain calcium or sulfur. By adding 2 tablespoons of gypsum (calcium sulfate) to each pound of fertilizer you have a nutrient blend suitable for hydro growing.

Since nitrogen, phosphorous and potassium make up 90% or more of most fertilizer blends, making up your own complete hydro fertilizer is not that tricky. Finding a source for each of these nutrients may be more difficult since most hydroponic stores prefer to sell high priced blends rather than inexpensive elements growers can mix themselves.

Here's how one grower mixed up a complete hydro nutrient blend for both vegetative growth and flowering. The basic fertilizer he used was Peters Professional Blossom Booster® which has an NPK of 10-30-20 and contains all the minor nutrients except sulfur and calcium. He could have used this fertilizer blend for flowering, as is, by adding a small amount of gypsum (calcium sulfate). Instead, he decided to use this blend as a base fertilizer for both vegetative and flowering. He wanted a fertilizer that would be taken up evenly by marijuana and that would need little pH adjustment when in solution.

He sent away for 50 pounds of calcium nitrate (15-0-0) plus 5% calcium. He also purchased 5 pounds of Peters® micro nutrient blend, which includes all the minor nutrients except calcium and magnesium. Other nutrients he used included gypsum (calcium sulfate), hydrated lime (calcium), and epsom salt (magnesium sulfate). These nutrients all cost considerably less than $1.00 per pound.

For vegetative growth he wanted a fertilizer blend somewhat high in nitrogen, and somewhat low in potassium. The formula he used was:

2 pounds Peters®	10-30-20
3 pounds Calcium Nitrate	15-0-0
1/4 cup epsom salt	
1/4 cup gypsum	
1 teaspoon) micro blend	

The epsom salt and micro blend are used to make the calcium nitrate a complete fertilizer. The gypsum rounds out the Peters® formula that lacks calcium and sulfur.

For flowering the formula is:

4 pounds Peters®	10-30-20
1 pound Calcium Nitrate	15-0-0
3/4 cup gypsum	
1 tablespoon epsom salt	
1/3 teaspoon micro blend	

If the nutrients are mixed in batches of about 5 or 10 pounds it is easy to figure out the NPK analysis of the fertilizer blend with a calculator. For the 5-pound batches above, the vegetative blend Peters® fertilizer makes up 40% of the blend, and the calcium nitrate 60%. To figure the NPK analysis, multiply the 10-30-20 NPK of the Peters® by .4, and multiply the 15-0-0 calcium nitrate by .6. Peters® comes out to 4-12-8, and the calcium nitrate 9-0-0. Add the two numbers together like this:

        4-12-8
        9- 0-0
        13-12-8

You find the fertilizer has an NPK of 13-12-8.

For flowering, the Peters® makes up about 80% of the blend, and the calcium nitrate 20%. In this case, multiply the NPK of the Peters® by .8, and the calcium nitrate by .2. Peters® comes out to 8-24-16, and the calcium nitrate 3-0-0. Add together like above:

        8-24-16
        3- 0- 0
        11-24-16

This flowering blend has an NPK of 11-24-16.

You can adjust the pH of these fertilizer blends to your local water conditions. By substituting hydrated lime for up to one half the gypsum, most growers can adjust the fertilizer so that it will have a suitable pH when mixed with water, without using **pH up** or **pH down.**

Growers can get deeper into fertilizer mixing, of course, by purchasing elemental forms of nitrogen, phosphorous, and potassium. Elemental phosphorous may be hard to find, however. Many forms of phosphorous include other nutrients. Ammonium phosphate, has nitrogen, for example, and potassium phosphate has potassium. Fertilizer companies often mix these chemicals together, and sell the mix as a flowering blend. Some liquid forms of phosphoric acid are available, but they are very acidic, dangerous to work with, and necessitate making the blend into a liquid.

You can see that, since such a small amount of micro-nutrient is needed for a complete fertilizer, it would be way too much work to try to mix your own micro-nutrient blend.

With the exception of nitrogen, both hydroponic and organic fertilizers are often derived from the same rock (mineral) sources.

Growers who want to mix their own nutrients should be sure the nutrients they are purchasing are easily dissolvable in water. Avoid nutrients that say they are "time released", which means they will release nutrients over time. Except for some outdoor and greenhouse applications, time released fertilizers are not suitable for hydro growing.

Organic Fertilizer

With the exception of nitrogen, both hydroponic and organic fertilizers are often derived from the same rock (mineral) sources. The difference is in how the minerals are treated once they are extracted from the source. Hydroponic fertilizers are treated with chemicals like sulfuric acid, which makes them immediately available for plant use. Hydro nutrients are also made to readily dissolve in water.

Organic forms of the same minerals are less treated, and are more slowly assimilated into the plant. Organic fertilizers are pulverized to various grades of powder. Fine powders are best for using in hydro units, both because they dissolve faster and are more quickly available to plants. Even so, organic nutrients are much slower in dissolving and becoming available as plant food.

Sources of nitrogen are the big difference between organic and hydro fertilizer. Nitrogen for hydro fertilizer is derived from natural gas. Organic nitrogen sources are made from decaying organic matter such as fish emulsion or bat guano. It's hard to say which source is better. Dried blood, for example, though a strong source of organic nitrogen is only as clean as the source. Cottonseed meal, another source of (slow acting) nitrogen, is made from the crop that gets the most pesticides.

That leaves fish emulsion (5-2-2) for an NPK source with a reasonably high analysis. Again, if you use this fertilizer, filtering is important, as fish scales will clog pumps. Many growers use panty hose to hold fertilizer, which they soak in the reservoir until most of the nutrients are dissolved. Fine sieves can also be used to filter out large particles. Fish fertilizer works pretty well but doesn't smell very good, which is not necessarily a bad thing. The fish stench helps cover the sweet smell of growing marijuana.

Getting organic nutrients into a good solution will increase the potency of the nutrient solution, and the amount available to the plants. Soaking organic nutrients in small amounts of hot water will increase fertilizer availability. Mix the nutrients in a small container with some hot water. If you can, put the covered nutrient in the sun for a couple of days. After that drain the nutrients through a fine sieve into the reservoir. Blenders can also help get organic nutrients ready for plant use. Organic nutrient tea can also be soaked in the reservoir if you can find a vessel that prevents large particles from getting into the reservoir water.

Several organic fertilizer companies sell nutrient activators, which are made up of various beneficial bacteria and enzymes. They are made to enhance the amount of nutrient available to the marijuana plants. Growers using hydro nutrients don't need activators since hydro nutrients are already in a form plants can use. Organic growers may find these activators helpful, however. Growers using an activator should see an upward spike in fertilizer levels, measured with a TDS meter, a day or so after adding an activator to the fertilizer brew, if it is effective.

Minor nutrients are added to organic fertilizer blends with products like Maxi Crop®, which is made from ground seaweed. Certain clays are available which also contain all of the micro-nutrients. Clay dissolves fairly well in hot water.

Don't try to use organic fertilizers without pH and dissolved solids meters. Fertilizer levels often increase over a number of days, especially when organic teas are soaked in the reservoir. Without the meters, growers have no idea what is available to the plants.

Another method of getting organic fertilizers to plants is through the growing media. Soil-based media, such as mushroom compost, are rich in nutrients and can be used by hydro growers. The trick to using soils for hydro growing is to mix them with other soil amendments, like medium and large size vermiculite.

Organic nutrients like greensand, fish meal, or rock phosphate can also be incorporated into the growing media in small amounts of 10-15%. These fertilizers will slowly release nutrients during the growing cycle.

Here are a few formulas for organic nutrient blends. They make 30 gallons.
Vegetative:

   2-3 cups fish emulsion
   1 cup high phosphate bat guano
   1/2 cup Maxi Crop®

Flower:

   2 cups fish emulsion
   2 cups high phosphate bat guano
   1/2 cup Maxi Crop®

You can substitute up to 1/2 cottonseed meal for fish emulsion in the above formulas. If you're in a kinky mood you can use blood fertilizer instead of fish. Blood is stronger than fish so you only use half as much.

Growing Media

Classic hydroponics has tended to use very small amounts of growing media, which sheds water quickly, so that the plant's roots receive copious amounts of air. This is great for grower who loves to tinker, because systems such as these are always operating close to the edge, and need constant maintenance. The less water the growing media holds, the quicker marijuana plants go down if there is a problem in the system. Quick drying media also mean the watering system has to operate more frequently, or even constantly, increasing the likelihood of problems.

Since the objective of the marijuana cultivator, (besides optimum growth), is a fail-safe growing system, some middle ground should be found. After all, most growers are not trying push the parameters of horticulture, they just want a dependable system of producing quality bud. They are interested in hydro systems with built in safeguards, not systems more at home in a sci-fi movie.

Plants in Rockwool Cubes

What we are talking about here is roots. Hydro systems such as aeroponics or nutrient film bathe the roots of marijuana with nutrient solution. In the darkness of the grow tubes these plants form a lavish root system. Having roots is pretty cool (and necessary), but the problem is that the roots are delicate and, once in place, the plants are hard to move around. Let's also not lose sight of the fact that marijuana growers are after flowers, not roots.

With this in mind we will look at growing media that holds air, water, and enough roots to keep the marijuana in top shape. Since the plants can be watered several times a day if needed, a lavish root system is rather superfluous.

Hydro growing media include popular items such as rockwool, and mixes containing volcanic rock, ceramic beads and horticultural products such as perlite and vermiculite. Organic media containing potting soil, mushroom compost, peat moss, coconut husks, or ground bark can also be used.

Here are a few blends for hydro growing media. The only medium that can be a problem in hydro growing is perlite, which floats and can clog pumps. Blended media may release small amounts of particulate into the reservoirs especially when new. Usually it does not cause problems. But do remove any debris that collects around drains. Thoroughly wetting the medium before use will help keep debris to a minimum.

Blend #1
> 3 parts volcanic rock or ceramic beads
> 1 part medium grade vermiculite, potting soil or mushroom compost

Blend #2
> 1 part potting soil
> 1 part medium grade vermiculite

Blend #3
>I part potting soil or mushroom compost
>I part medium grade vermiculite
>I part ground bark

Blend #4
>I part potting soil
>I part coconut husks or peat moss
>2 parts medium grade vermiculite
>I part ground bark

The name of the game for mixed media is aggregate size. Growers want a medium that holds water, but also has larger pieces that allow it to drain well.

The name of the game for mixed media is aggregate size. Growers want a medium that holds water, but also has larger pieces that allow it to drain well. This prevents the medium from becoming soggy, and allows good air penetration. Potting soil, for example, usually holds too much water and not enough air to be used as a hydro medium. Mixing the soil with intermediate-sized vermiculite and/or ground bark will make the medium more suitable for hydro applications. Soil can also be mixed with volcanic rock or ceramic beads.

Rockwool is the most popular hydro growing medium. It is made up of spun filaments of rock. Rockwool hold lots of water, and also allows good air penetration to the roots. Ease of transplanting clones, and the fact that containers are not needed, if rockwool cubes are used, also make this medium popular. The cubes also work well with the very reliable flood and drain system.

A 4-inch square rockwool cube holds enough water to sustain a 4-foot marijuana plant for at least one day. This gives the grower some time to detect any problems in the growing system. Larger cubes hold more water, of course.

Rockwool slabs, long pieces of rockwool encased in a plastic bag, are sometimes used for growing marijuana, usually with drip systems. Slabs do hold lots of water, so much that they are heavy and hard to move when saturated. For the way marijuana is usually grown indoors, where plants usually finish at 4 feet or under, rockwool slabs seem like overkill. For smaller plants like these the slabs are too wet. Slabs make more sense if full-grown plants are desired.

For all its pluses, the rockwool medium does require special handling. Because the rock filaments are alkaline, the pH of the nutrient solution used must be adjusted, for best results. Initially the rockwool cubes are soaked overnight in water brought to pH 5. There are special conditioners for rockwool, but **pH down** or bloom fertilizers can also be used. Thereafter the nutrient solution is mixed to an acidic pH of 5.5-5.8.

Some growers use baled rockwool, which is stuffed into containers. This rockwool also needs conditioning. Wetting baled rockwool with pH 5 water before use is recommended. This conditioning also makes the rockwool easier to use, as dry rockwool releases a glassine dust, which is irritating to the skin and lungs. As with cubes, the nutrient solution should be mixed at pH 5.5 - 5.8.

Baled rockwool can also be mixed with about 30-40% peat moss, which has an acidic pH of about 5.5. This effectively counters the alkalinity of the rockwool. Nutrient solutions in the pH 6-6.5 range are used for growing.

The water holding capacity of rockwool is usually a big plus. For a few applications though, such as cloning, rockwool holds too much water when it is completely saturated. Rockwool can be used for cloning if it is pH conditioned and wet but not totally saturated. This is a little tricky, but can be done by weight, and it is relatively easy to get the knack. When soaked, rockwool will quickly become saturated. To drain some of this water out, place one wet cube on top of another. The water from the top cube will quickly drain out into the one on the bottom.

One other downside to using rockwool can occur if the wool dries out. Rockwool quickly pulls water out of the plants when it dries, making the plants wilt. Plants can be revived only for a short time.

Chapter 5

Strategic Growing Tips

The methods used to grow marijuana indoors under lights are significantly different from growing it outdoors. Using hydro is only one of the methods that have made indoor growing viable. These techniques include several easy-to-implement concepts. Because of these developments, the best marijuana available now is often grown indoors.

The concepts that have been developed for the indoor grow center on the fact that marijuana can be induced to flower at any point in its' growing cycle under lights. Flowering is as simple as adjusting the light and darkness cycles to 12 hours each. Since electric lights are not suitable for flowering full-grown, full-height marijuana, much smaller plants are used indoors. Smaller plants make good use of the light that is available.

Short, young plants are the foundation of the "Sea of Green" growing method, where many smaller plants, each having equal space, are used.

Short, young plants are the foundation of the **"Sea of Green"** growing method, where many smaller plants, each having equal space, are used. The marijuana is usually induced to flower when it reaches 2 to 3 feet in height. At 2 feet up to 30 plants will fit under a 1000-watt light. Growers who want to keep the plant count down can use plants up to 3 feet; about 20 will fit under the same light.

Because an indoor grower can flower the marijuana at will, systems have been developed to grow crops continuously. Small **feeder systems** can be used to grow the marijuana to the height desired for flowering. When ready, the marijuana is moved to the flowering area. Kind of like "just in time" horticulture. Some marijuana plants are being propagated and grown in the vegetative state at the same time other plants are flowering under the high intensity light. Crops can be harvested every couple of months with this technique.

Feeder systems need not be large. Three hundred watts of fluorescent lights, for example, can produce enough plant to supply a 1000-watt flowering system. The feeder system will also have enough space to root cuttings, which makes seeds unnecessary.

Continuously-producing systems are a real achievement made possible largely by automated growing, and an understanding of what triggers the marijuana plant to flower. However, growing systems that are always running can pose a few problems. Growing the same crop (and often the same plant, if cuttings are propagated) over and over can lead to insect, bacteria or viral buildup. Growers with a single crop are not likely to have these problems unless they bring in sick or infected plants. Over time though, odds are higher that some kind of sickness will occur. See chapter 8, which deals with pests. What I want to talk about here is a cultural practice that can help the grower beat the odds.

With feeder systems, marijuana plants can be moved to the flowering area in two ways: all at once, or periodically, when they reach a certain height, for example. A flowering room with several lights will always have marijuana plants in different stages of flowering, if plants are moved into the room at different times. This makes it much more difficult to clean the growing area between crops since there will always be live plants there. A clean growing area is necessary to avoid problems in a continuously running garden. The best way to achieve this is to set up the garden so that it can be harvested all at once. Then spend a day cleaning the grow room before putting in the new crop. This practice will help prevent problems, or minimize them should they occur.

Clone Zone

Cuttings or clones are used to propagate prize female plants. They are made by rooting branches of a plant chosen for some exceptional characteristic, such as high yield, quick ripening, good fragrance, or resistance to disease.

With cloning, every plant is a genetic replica of the plant from which the cutting was taken. Because only female plants are usually cloned, growers no longer need to use seeds, which will grow 50% male plants as well as female.

Some cultivators grow out a cutting, and continuously take clones from it. This is called a "mother plant". Cuttings can also be taken from the bottom branches of plants, just before they are flowered. Cuttings root more easily if the marijuana is not flowering, but most cuttings will root even if taken from a plant that is 3 to 4 weeks into flowering.

One relatively foolproof method of cloning is the **fish tank** method. A fish tank, outfitted with an aerator and heater, is used for rooting the cuttings. A small fluorescent fixture is hung above the tank for light. The cuttings are poked through styrofoam boats, "to go" restaurant trays, and floated on the fish tank filled with water. A small fish tank can root 60 or more clones at a time.

Fish Tank Clones

The water in the tank should be conditioned to a slightly acidic pH, 6.5, for best results. Rooting compound can be added to the water in the tank. A small amount of nutrient, 400 ppm, can also be added to the water. The water is kept at 80°F with a heater, and is replenished as needed. Once the marijuana develops stubby roots (2 weeks) break up the styrofoam to remove the cuttings. Then, transplant. Another cloning technique is described in next chapter, Marijuana on Line.

Pruning plants just before the marijuana is put int
flowering has been mentioned as a method of obtainin
material for clones. Pruning plants correctly can als
increase yield, and make plants easier to trim at harves
The concept here is that the heaviest flowering will occu
within a few feet of the light. The branches at the bottor
of the plant will be relatively non-productive. If thes
branches are removed, the plant puts its energy int
producing larger flowers at the top of the plant.

On a 2-foot marijuana plant ready to flower, 6-8 branche
are left on the top of the plant. All other branches a
removed. To open the top of the plant to light, the larg
fan leaves are also removed wherever a branch has formec
Fan leaves grow from the main stem where these branche
form. Fan leaves are use to shield the plant from ver
intense sun. Marijuana plants will also draw nutrients fror
these leaves if the plant is under-fertilized. Well-fertilize
indoor plants are not subject to these conditions. All th
fan leaves do in this case is shade the buds so they don
develop as well.

Marijuana plants enjoy a good pruning, if yield an
quality of flowers is any indication. Marijuana grow
rapidly even when flowering, and after a few weeks th
plants will begin crowding each other. Many growers prun
again at this time. Keeping the canopy of the garden ope
assures good light will strike the flowering sights on th
marijuana plant. This is how growers cultivate larg
flowers on small plants.

Pruned plants produce as well or better than unprune
plants. The flowers on pruned plants are larger and easi
to manicure at harvest. Another plus to pruning plants i
that insect infestations often start on lower plant leave:
Removing lower branches slows down any burgeoning ir
festation. If the lower branches of a marijuana plant are clea
they can also be used for cuttings, to propagate a new crof

One other concept that is easy to implement and improve
yield is **plant placement.** Plants are placed under the light

Hydro Buds

Season of Green

Greenhouse Dreams

The Great Outdoors

High and Dry

so that a good amount of light strikes every plant. Taller plants, or plants that stretch a lot after flowering is initiated are located around the outside of growing area: a stadium-like set up.

A grid system of placement, with plants spaced at equal distance from each other, is often used. Equal space for each plant by using a grid works well but plants should also be positioned so that no plant shades another. Plant supports, as discussed previously, are used to keep the marijuana upright so that plants don't fall on each other as the heavy buds mature.

Pruned Plants Before and After

Chapter 6

The final piece of setting up is operating the system. It would be confusing to describe all the different kinds of hydroponic systems. Our study will be of one grower's ebb & flow (flood & drain) system because it is easy to set up and operates very dependably. Much of the information will be relevant to growers using other systems, such as aeroponics or drip systems. Variations on the systems are described in the first chapter.

The ebb & flow system we are looking at was set up on hand made tables, 32 inches off the ground, and big enough to hold two 4x4 foot trays. Each table is equipped with one 1000-watt or two 600-watt high pressure sodium lights. A 32-gallon trash can is used as a reservoir for each tray. It is connected to the tray with 1/2 inch connectors and flexible tubing. The tubing carries the nutrient solution to the trays, and then back to the reservoir at the end of the watering cycle. A 15-gallon-per-minute submersible pump is connected on the reservoir end of the tubing. On the tray side the tubing is connected to a fitting that is screwed onto the tray and filters debris out of the nutrient solution.

Ebb & flow system using rockwool cubes showing trays and reservoirs. A single pipe delivers water and drains the trays.

Each table is connected to 2 timers: one to operate the lights and one, a digital timer, which controls several pumps. Several tables are connected to each timer. A wired-in high-capacity timer is used for the lights. The digital timer gives the grower the flexibility to run the watering system as needed. This grower gives the marijuana the minimum amount of water needed to keep the plants in top condition.

A single watering cycle of 4-5 minutes per day is used on small plants, enough so that the water gets a couple of inches deep in the tray before draining back into the reservoir. Up to 6 cycles per day may be used on large, fast-growing marijuana plants. More typically, 3 watering cycles are adequate. The grower determines exactly how many watering cycles to program by lifting the rockwool, and judging watering needs by its' weight. With a system on three watering cycles a day, the cycles are programmed to occur just before the lights turn on, and every four hours thereafter. The plants are not watered during the night cycle.

All the timers are plugged into a ground fault circuit interrupter, to prevent shocks and shut off the system if an electrical malfunction occurs.

The lights used by the grower in the flowering area are 1000-watt high-pressure sodium lights. The lights are mounted vertically in huge parabolic reflectors, 4 feet in diameter. The grower picked these lights after much experimentation. The primary consideration was the yield, which is significantly better under these lights. He was also able to avoid putting the light on light movers. This was a safety consideration for the grower even though light movers have a good safety record.

The system uses selected clones derived from skunk and hybrid skunk varieties of marijuana. A separate "feeder system" is used to grow the clones until they are big enough to flower. The feeder system is in continuous light (24 hours a day) so that the plants rapidly grow to the 10-15 inch height the grower wants before flowering is initiated. Twenty to thirty plants are used for each tray when flowering.

Fluorescent lights are used to root the cuttings, which are subsequently grown under metal halide lights. Once the marijuana reaches the required height and has developed a strong stem, it is moved to a flowering room with high-pressure sodium lights, which are on 12 hours a day.

Cuttings rooting under fluorescent lights. Six cuttings are stuck in each 4 inch cube. When rooted, the clones are cut apart and each is put into its own cube.

Most of the marijuana plants are less than 3 feet high at harvest. Each plant yields only up to 1 ounce (28 grams) of prime flowers, but the yield per light is high. The grower averages 1.5 pounds (680 grams) per 1000-watt light, with 30-40 plants per light.

The clones were selected for the high as well as the growth pattern and yield of the plant. The clones that stretch or elongate most when in flowering are placed on the outside of the tray so they won't shade plants that grow more slowly. This is known as the "stadium effect" and it uses light very efficiently.

The walls of the growing area are surrounded by mirror-like Mylar@ to reflect light back to the plants that would otherwise escape the growing area. Other walls were white-washed with somewhat less effect.

This system uses 4 inch conditioned rockwool cubes for the plants. The cubes make it very easy to transplant clones, with little possibility of transplant shock. The cubes are conditioned in a trashcan of water treated with a few table-spoons of phosphoric acid. They are soaked in this pH 4.5 solution overnight. Rockwool cubes were selected because they hold up to a day's worth of water should the system go down. Not having to use containers was also a prime consideration.

Because the system uses rockwool cubes, the grower uses a nutrient solution on the acidic side, 5.5 to 5.8 on the pH scale. He monitors the nutrient solution with a pH meter and adjusts it with a ready-made solution of pH down (phosphoric acid).

Clones are also rooted in these 4-inch cubes, 6 cuttings to a cube. The grower favors the 4-inch cubes over the small 1-inch cubes sold for starting clones or seeds. The grower has found that cubes that are not totally saturated with water work best. It is easy to drain water out of the larger cubes by placing one wet cube on top of the other. In a few seconds, much of the water from the top cube drains into the bottom cube.

Rooted clones just planted in rockwool cubes.

To keep the rockwool cubes at the preferred 1/2 saturation the grower uses hand watering on this part of the system. Eight cubes fit into the standard 11x17 inch plastic gardening tray. The grower determines when to water by lifting the end of the tray, and seeing how heavy the cubes are. The clones use more water as they begin to root.

The grower dips each cutting into a rooting gel before they are stuck into the rockwool cubes. Rooting gels are all made of an auxin-like plant hormone known to enhance the rooting of clones. Small amounts of fertilizer, 200-300 ppm, are used in the water for the clones. The clones are ready for transplanting in 2-3 weeks. The 4-inch cubes are cut apart with a plastic knife, and each clone plugged into its own 4-inch cube.

Relatively large pieces of plants are used for cloning although any branchwith a growing tip will work. Large pieces are preferred because they tend to grow with less branching and a larger stem. Since the grower removes branches that are likely to be non-productive before putting them into flowering this saves time.

Because the plants become top-heavy late in flowering a plastic grid is used to support the plants when they are heavy with bud. The grid, plastic fencing in this case, is hung about 2 feet above the table. The marijuana plants grow up through the grid as they get larger. Plant supports are very important. Without support, the plants tend to grow bigger stems instead of bigger buds.

The grower uses ready-made liquid fertilizer that is sold in three parts, one for vegetative growth (high nitrogen), one for flowering (high phosphate), and one including the micronutrients. The micronutrients are used with both the flowering and vegetative fertilizer blends. The grower uses a dissolved solids meter to measure the amount of fertilizer in the nutrient solution. He starts with about a cup (8 fluid ounces) of nutrients dissolved in 30 gallons of water, and adjusts the solution from there. Small plants get about 800 ppm (parts per million) as measured by the meter. Larger plants get up to 1500 ppm.

Reservoirs are filled and adjusted on a weekly basis, especially when the plants get large. Rich nutrient solutions tend to spike upward as plants use the water and excess nutrients are left behind. A 1200 ppm nutrient solution may measure up to 2000 ppm after a week of use. Nutrient solutions over 2500 ppm will damage marijuana plants. Reservoirs are emptied, cleaned, and refilled about every two months between crops.

This grower uses a closed ventilation system, which is seldom vented to the outside. To do this the grower feeds the marijuana carbon dioxide gas (CO_2) from tanks. The gas is essential to plant growth and is taken in by the leaves of the plant. An air conditioner, set on re-circulate is also used to keep the temperature in the grow room in the optimum range of 80-85° F.

Plant supports are very important. Without support, the plants tend to grow bigger stems instead of bigger buds.

The air conditioner also acts as a dehumidifier removing water from the air of the growing area. Keeping humidity below 70%, especially late in the flowering stage, helps prevent problems like mold formation. The air conditioner produces a small amount of water, which is recycled back to a reservoir, with a small pipe. The heat the machine produces is vented out of the grow area.

The CO_2 is released into the growing area from a metal tank. A CO_2 kit, sold at hydro stores, releases the gas at a set rate from the tank. CO_2 levels are monitored by a relatively expensive CO_2 meter and are kept at 1000-1200 ppm, 3-4 times the amount found in the air around us. The CO_2 comes on 1 hour before the lights are turned on, and is shut off an hour before the lights are turned off. In a room containing 3 lights using 3000 watts the grower releases 1/2 cubic foot of CO_2 every hour the lights are on.

Both vegetative and flowering growth is rapid because of the CO_2. Some marijuana varieties flower in as little as six weeks. The grower delivers the CO_2 to the marijuana through a small pipe connected to a control unit that screws on to the tank of CO_2 gas. It is blown around the growing room with a fan.

Fans are also used to send cool air from the air conditioner into the grow area. Interior ventilation mitigates potential problems like mold formation, which can be a problem in muggy growing areas. Moving air makes it more difficult for mold and insect problems to get started.

Even with the controls, fans and air conditioner, the grow area, since it contains several lights, occasionally becomes over-heated. On the few days that the temperature rises over 90°F the grower turns off the lights for a few hours during the worst of the heat, and leaves the air conditioner on. Since this happens very seldom it is not a big problem. In warmer areas of the country during summer over-heating may be more of a problem. A large air conditioner may be needed to grow during the hottest months.

Air conditioner and carbon dioxide tank.

Since the grow room is in an area of the country that seldom gets heavy frost, it seldom goes below 60°F (the temperature that inhibits flower formation in most varieties of marijuana) at night. When it does, the grower uses a dehumidifier as a heater. The dehumidifier also removes water from the grow room air, allowing the grower to keep the system "closed" (not vented to the outside). The dehumidifier is used during the dark cycle, when the lights are off. The grower does not need added heat when the lights are on, since the lights are so hot.

Day-to-day operation of this system includes a number of easy tasks that keep the system operating at peak efficiency. Getting the marijuana clones ready for flowering is a large part of the operation. About 250 clones are kept in vegetative growth. About 3000 watts of light are used in the vegetative part of the system. The lights are on full time, 24 hours a day.

Everybody needs a plan

Turnover in plants is rapid. Often the trays are refilled with new plants on the same day they are emptied and the older plants are harvested. The trays are washed with a solution of hydrogen peroxide between crops. The cleaning water is sponged out of the trays for cleanliness, but the little peroxide that may get into the reservoir is not dangerous, it adds oxygen to the water.

Decisions on when to harvest are based on several factors and are subjective. When seedless marijuana begins to ripen, the seedpods begin to swell as if they contained seeds. Resin accumulates on these seedless pods. The hair like *cilia* on the flowers, which would collect pollen if there were male plants around, begin to change color from white to a rusty red. Once all the pods are swollen and resin-encrusted the grower begins to harvest. Plants that mature more slowly may be left in the flowering area for up to a week to ripen.

For all the automation used in this grow, the grower credits his success to all the hand work he invests in a crop.

Another factor affecting harvest times is the weather. If it is going to be extremely cold, hot, or rainy, the grower may harvest the crop a few days early rather than risk humidity problems. Since mature plants expel a lot of water through transpiration, greatly adding to the humidity in the growing area, the plants are more susceptible to flower molding. If for any reason the grower does not think he can control the situation, the plants are harvested. Telltale browning of leaves and flowers are a sign that the mold process is taking hold.

Even under ideal conditions the grower likes to pick when the plants are just ripe and aromatic. He prefers the cool sweet taste of the flowers when they are in this stage. The flowers could be left for up to 2 more weeks and will add slightly more weight. The smoke from these plants will often be stronger tasting and likely to make a person cough. Little difference in potency was noticed with different harvesting times.

The plants are trimmed as soon as they are harvested. Plants that are trimmed while the leaves are still turgid are much easier to work with than semi-dry plants whose leaves are drooping. After the plants have been trimmed, they are dried. Besides removing water from plants, drying also removes small amounts of chlorophyll from the flowers.

Because of the volume of plant material the grower processes he has constructed a small drying room, equipped with a dehumidifier. Humidity is kept in the 40-50% range. Large flowers are hung to dry while small buds are dried on shelves covered with plastic screening to improve air circulation around and under the buds. A couple of days before drying is complete, about 5-7 days into the process, the grower piles the flowers together, which slightly cures them. The flowers lose a little chlorophyll and turn less green. They are soon ready for use.

For all the automation used in this grow, the grower credits his success to all the hand work he invests in a crop. The grower spends much time, making cuttings, transplanting and placing plants so that they receive maximum light. Getting things just right pays off. After all, the marijuana plant is living thing. Automation is used to keep the plants in prime condition, not to change them into THC machines.

Once all the pods are swollen and resin-encrusted the grower begins to harvest.

Chapter 7 Pestilence

"Shit happens" as the famous bumper sticker opines. If anything, this book is an attempt to explore ways of setting up dependable growing systems and avoiding problems. Still, growers are working with a living organism, the marijuana plant. Not only that, but many growers cultivate successive crops, sometimes over many years, in the same location. Even with the best of care, problems such as insects or disease will pay an unwelcome visit one day.

Still, most problems start because of something the grower does inadvertently. The grower may come across some great clones, for example, and put them in the growing area without thoroughly examining the leaves for insects. A growing area may be consistently operated in high humidity and slack ventilation, setting off a mold or insect attack. Not that critters can't find their way into the growing area, even without your help.

There are three ways of fighting pests and plant diseases. One is cultivation practice, such as setting up the space so it can be easily cleaned between crops. The other two are beneficial insects or organisms and finally, chemicals. All are important in controlling the problem. Organic controls have improved markedly, and for the most part are just as effective as toxic chemicals. Even so, disposable dust masks and eye protection should be used when applying any pesticide, organic or otherwise. Always turn off the grow lights when spraying plants.

Finding the problem early is essential; both for the outcome of the current crop, and to minimize the work needed to eliminate the problem. If an insect problem is discovered early, for example, a few sprayings may eliminate them. Unchecked, pests can shut down a grow, and necessitate a major cleaning and new stock to get the unit back on line.

A small magnifying glass is helpful in determining which bug is attacking. Periodically removing any yellowing or spotted leaves and examining their undersides with the magnifier will help detect insect outbreaks at the beginning.

SPIDER MITES

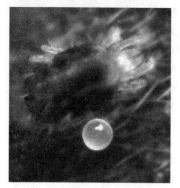

Mite & Webs on Plant

This relative of the spider, the two-spotted mite, strikes fear in the heart of marijuana growers. Mites can get into the growing area in several ways. Often they are brought into the area from clones brought in from the outside. Certain houseplants often harbor sizable populations of spider mites. Outdoor gardens of plants (other than marijuana) may also have small populations of mites that do little visible damage. A cultural practice used by many marijuana cultivators is not to work in other regular gardens before entering the grow rooms. This will help prevent these buggers from hitching a ride to the indoor marijuana garden. Pets can also bring insects into the growing area.

Mites feed by sucking sap from leaves with a sharp little proboscis. This makes small holes in the leaves, leaving a small pinpoint dot. Spotted leaves, usually starting on the bottom of the plant, are the first sign that mites have arrived. Examining the underside of the leaf with a magnifying glass will confirm your suspicions.

Once mites are detected it is important to determine how bad the infestation is. The mites will eventually weave webs, and this indicates a heavy infestation. Growers must also decide how likely it is that the infestation can be eliminated. With quick action the plants can be gotten through to harvest. But if the clones and breeding stock are highly infested a major clean out may be needed - possibly including bringing in new stock.

The first line of defense against mites is pyrethrum spray. This is an organic pesticide derived from chrysanthemums. Because mites are very small, aerosol-like sprays are most effective. A small pump sprayer can also deliver a mist of small droplets, which are difficult for the mites to avoid. Thoroughly wet the underside of leaves for best results.

Pyrethrums are somewhat toxic to plants so, if plants are in vegetative growth, you may want to let them recover from the mites and the spray before moving them to the flowering area.

Pyrethrums should not be used more than once every three weeks. If you get pyrethrums that are to be mixed with water, use 75% of recommended dosage to see how plants react. One spraying will not eliminate mites because mite eggs will still be viable. These eggs hatch at 3-5 day intervals.

A holding action against mites may be the only possibility until the present crop is harvested. After harvest, the flowering area should be thoroughly cleaned. Washing and spraying the growing area with chlorine bleach, ammonia, or hydrogen peroxide will kill any remaining eggs. All these products are fairly toxic and should not be used around live plants. Never mix any of these chemicals together. None of the three should be used without a respirator and protective clothing.

Chlorine bleach is probably the most toxic of these three cleaners. Chlorine is a gas so the area should be closed off once it is sprayed. Never mix chlorine bleach with other cleaners, particularly ammonia. Ventilate the area before re-entering.

Ammonia and hydrogen peroxide are less toxic than chlorine bleach in that any leftover residues are not harmful to marijuana plants. Ammonia is mostly nitrogen, a plant nutrient. Hydrogen peroxide will break down to hydrogen and oxygen. Even so, they should not be used around live plants.

Two other organic products are helpful in fighting mites. The first is a new product, a fungus that that attacks and kills mites called *Beauvenia bassiana*. Two companies are marketing this fungus: Botanigard® is sold by Mycotech Co., and Naturalis T&O® by Bioworks Inc. Both companies have web sites, which include a dealer list that is helpful because these products are new and not always readily available. These products kill the three major insects that attack marijuana: mites, white flies, and thrips.

The fungi work well and do not heavily damage plants or clones. They also work well in conjunction with pyrethrum sprays. Use one spray of pyrethrum to kill live mites, and then follow up a few days later with a spray of the fungus. Several sprays of this fungus should be applied to eliminate mites.

Another way to eliminate mites is a predatory mite, which eats the eggs of the spider mite. Predatory mites will not work on flowering plants because they need long days to flourish. They are very effective on marijuana plants in vegetative growth and clones. Most grow stores can order these mites for you.

One other natural insecticide that is fairly effective against mites is cinnamon oil. Use 1 teaspoon in a quart of water with a little soap or detergent to disperse the oil in the water.

Cultural practices are also important in preventing mites. As was mentioned, being able to clean an area becomes important once infestation occurs. To do this, at some point the growing area has to be empty. Mite populations expand rapidly in warm stagnant air. A well ventilated grow space with air moving over the marijuana plants makes it hard for mite populations to get going. Because mites often infest lower portion of plants first, pruning plants before moving them from vegetative growth to flowering will often reveal early infestations, when they are easier to eliminate. Pruning the bottom branches of marijuana plants is also used to reduce infestations. Some growers use these branches for cloning, when they are free of bugs.

WHITE FLY

This tiny fly with white wings can do real damage to greenhouse, and electric light grown marijuana. They suck sap from the bottom of the plants' leaves. White flies can enter growing areas easily because they can fly. Contaminated clones are another likely source of infestations. Fortunately this pest is relatively easy to snuff, if caught early. Good ventilation, and moderate temperatures discourage heavy infestations.

Yellow sticky traps attract this insect and they become stuck to the traps' surface. The traps won't stop an infestation, but are used to indicate a problem. Soil gnats, which don't have the telltale white wings, also become entangled in these traps.

A single spray of pyrethrums can take out a small infestation of white flies because it also kills the eggs. Larger infestations may need a second spraying. The beneficial fungus, *Beauvenia bassiana*, contained in the products, Botanigard® and Naturalis T&O® (see above) will also eliminate white flies in a few sprayings. It is important to eradicate white flies as soon as they are found because they can carry plant viruses, which may attack marijuana plants. These viruses can weaken breeding stock and flowering plants. Some viruses, like fusarian wilt, can be fatal to susceptible marijuana plants.

THRIPS

Not as damaging as mites and white flies, thrips can be difficult to eliminate entirely. Their life cycle includes an egg stage and a larval stage, when they feed on the bottom of leaves. Later they grow wings and fly off to infest other parts of your garden.

Pyrethrum and soap sprays do a fairly good job of controlling thrips infestations. Botanigard® or Naturalis T&O® will also control this pest. The only problem is that thrips may reenter the grow rooms from the outside, which is the usual way they enter a garden. Thrips infect the bottom leaves of the marijuana plant first so pruning plants is an effective aid in controlling this insect.

APHIDS

Dead aphid walking.

Fat little sap sucking insects, aphids are not usually a major problem for marijuana plants. A small number of each brood of aphids will form wings so they can enter grow rooms, usually setting off a minor infestation. Small numbers of aphids can be killed by hand, or with a soap spray.

The other way aphids get around is by being carried by ants. Ants actually carry aphids onto plants, and collect the digested sap the aphids suck from the plants' leaves. Infestations set off by ants can be serious. You have to stop the ants to stop the aphids. Ants can live in organic growing media, but usually in hydro-style growing too much water is run through the medium for ants to colonize it.

More likely a long line of ants can be found entering the grow room. Some growers use commercially available ant poisons because they will not be applied to plants. Ant poisons are toxic and persistent, however.

Organic detergents like Simple Green® will kill ants on contact. Follow the line of ants as far as possible. If you find a likely nest it can be flooded with water, which may bring thousands of ants to the surface, where they can be sprayed.

Cinnamon also deters ants. Dust it around likely entry points for the ants. Once the ants are deterred any remaining aphids can be killed with soap sprays.

MOTHS

During certain times of the year moths may enter grow rooms, where they lay eggs on the leaves of marijuana plants. The eggs hatch into larvae or caterpillars that can be fairly large, depending on the variety. They can munch large holes in marijuana leaves, and very quickly do a large amount of damage to plants.

Fortunately, they are easy to render dead. An organic pesticide called BT, for *Bacillus Thuregensis*, is a beneficial bacterium that attacks insects in the larvae stage. BT is very effective against moth larvae and pretty easy to find.

Soap sprays and pyrethrums are effective on flying moths.

MEALY BUGS

Not usually a problem on marijuana grown for short periods and forced to flower, mealy bugs occasionally attack full size, long season plants. Greenhouse growers are most likely to experience an attack by these lice-like insects. Removing infected leaves is a fairly effective way to fight infestations, as are pyrethrum sprays.

RODENTS

Stoner rats and mice sometimes attack marijuana, usually young plants. Edible toxic poisons like Decon® are effective. They are very toxic but don't usually come in contact with plants. Traps, baited with peanut butter, are organic and effective.

DEER

Deer, elk, and even moose will feed on marijuana plants outdoors. Often fencing, made of chicken wire, is the only way to keep them out of the grow area. Indoor growers usually do not face such large wildlife problems.

HELICOPTERS

Man-made mechanical bugs are a real problem in some areas. Whirly birds are used to find both outdoor and indoor gardens. Hiding outdoor gardens is a major consideration for the grower. The grower might keep the stands of marijuana small, or prune the plants so they don't have the typical conical shape. Cultivated spots in the middle of nowhere are made to blend in to the surroundings so as not to tip off to the sky spies.

Helicopters are used in some areas to detect heat coming from buildings with infrared cameras. Fortunately these cameras are ineffective during daylight hours. Some indoor growers adjust the light-cycle given to plants because of this.

A Fungus Among Us

More insidious than insects, fungi and plant viruses usually crop up when the same strain of marijuana is grown for prolonged periods in the same place. Not all of these organisms are "bad apples". Good fungi and bacteria, for example, break down soil and nutrients and make them available as food for the plants. Unfortunately, similar organisms can attack living plants.

Most often infection by these micro-organisms occurs over a period of time. The organism builds up to detrimental levels only when conditions are right. Fungi reproduce by spores, which may be present in small amounts in most grows. Bad growing conditions determine if an infection will get going. Improper ventilation, temperatures, or high humidity can set off an attack. Over watering, or a growing media that is not well aerated are also common causes of infection. Major insect infestations can set off a secondary infection with these micro-organisms.

PYTHIUM

Over watering, or a growing media that is not well aerated are also common causes of infection.

Pythium is a fungus that can attack marijuana plants in two ways. "Damping off", where marijuana grown from seed suddenly keels over and croaks is caused by pythium. The stem of the seedling disintegrates where it emerges from the growing medium. Over watering and poor air circulation encourages damping off.

Dusting seeds with a fungicide like Captan® is a technique used by many growers. Captan® is not organic but is safer than most fungicides, and very small amounts are used.

The *pythium* fungus can also cause problems as plants get larger. The fungus causes root rot, a condition often fatal to marijuana. The plants wilt as though they lack water, lose leaves, and then bite the dust. An examination of the plant just below the medium line will reveal a browning of the roots, which are normally white. The roots become clogged so that water and nutrients cannot freely move throughout the plant.

Root rot is always set off by bad growing practices, mainly over-watering and/or a soggy growing medium. Changing these practices can solve the problem. Cut the number of watering cycles immediately. While the media is drying, the plants can be sprayed with water to keep them from wilting. Use a different media that holds less water and more air on subsequent crops. The growing area should be cleaned thoroughly before a new crop is started.

Mycotech, mentioned above, markets a product called Root Shield®, which is fairly effective against root rot. Root Shield® contains a beneficial fungus and is considered organic. Though fairly expensive it can save a crop. Root Shield® can also be used on cuttings by dipping the clones in the powder. It seems to help clones root faster.

MILDEW

Powdery mildew infects the leaves of marijuana plants. White patches, which are spores, appear on the plant's leaves and sometimes the stem. Poor ventilation allows this fungus to take hold. The fungus does well in the temperatures favorable for growing marijuana.

Sulfur sprays are effective against mildew. Growers should increase the ventilation in the infected area. A breeze over the plants inhibits spore germination. Lowering the humidity in the grow is also helpful.

MOLD

This bacteria always appears at the exactly the wrong time, when the flowers are just about ripe. The spores feed off the sugars in the ripening bud. Low temperatures, lack of sufficient light, high humidity, and slack ventilation all encourage mold. Mold can be a problem on both indoor and outdoor plants.

Outdoors, many growers begin harvest at the first sign of mold, unless the weather is going to improve. Cutting out infected buds may give the grower a few more days of grow time. Indoor growers may also remove infected flowers, but ventilation and heat should be increased to inhibit new spore formation.

At harvest, separate infected flowers out from the rest. Keep in mind that even flowers that are seemingly uninfected may contain spores. If the crop is to be saved for long term use, dry it well and store it in the freezer.

WILTS

Verticillium wilt sometimes attacks marijuana plants, and infects plants through the growing medium. The plant begins wilting on the bottom leaves and eventually the condition worsens. In some cases the plant is dispatched to the great beyond.

Fortunately, *verticillium* usually only attacks a few plants from a crop. Nonetheless, it may be wise to look for a new variety of marijuana to grow, once *verticillium* is on board, because it can build up over time. Discard the old growing medium and change to a new mix for new crops.

VIRUSES

A number of viruses attack marijuana, but usually don't kill. They can inhibit good plant growth. A host of symptoms, usually some malformation of the leaves, or stunted plants indicate a viral sickness if growing conditions are otherwise good. Clones and cuttings, for example, are reported to "run down" over time by many growers. Rather than running down, the marijuana has probably picked up a virus.

Since there is no cure for this condition, bringing in new stock and deep cleaning the growing space is indicated.

*Greenhouse marijuana planted late
in the season, using rockwool slabs
and a drip system.*

Chapter 8

Greenhouses

Greenhouse gardening is the most popular new form of horticulture in the USA. This is because many kits for constructing greenhouses are available at relatively inexpensive prices. It's not surprising that a few wiseacres out there are growing marijuana in some of these greenhouses.

Greenhouse hydro systems are varied depending on how large the grower wants the marijuana plants to be. Most often, large, full-season marijuana is grown, flowering in autumn much like outdoors. The plants are grown in large containers or in conditioned soil in the ground. Water and nutrients are fed to the plants through drip lines.

Other growers, who are more sophisticated, have set up systems that can trick marijuana plants into flowering at any time. This is known as flower forcing. As we have seen, marijuana growers using lights are able to make plants flower simply by giving them equal periods (12 hours) of light and darkness each day. Indoors, this is as simple as setting a timer. Greenhouse growers have come up with more elaborate systems to do the same thing. They use blackout shades, for example, to give the marijuana the 12 hours of darkness required for flowering to occur. They also know that most varieties of marijuana will flower if it is put in the greenhouse anytime from late August until the end of March the following year.

Flowering greenhouse plants

Hydro greenhouse growers using flower forcing techniques can set up in much the same way as growers using lights, with tables, trays and the other equipment mentioned in previous chapters. This assumes the marijuana plants will be harvested while relatively small, 6 feet or less.

One Way Drip

The hydro method most often used by greenhouse growers is to automate the watering system, using drip lines. Often the water is not re-circulated back to a reservoir. This is known as the one-way drip system. These systems are easy to set up both for container gardening and for plants grown in the ground. This method is usually used on plants started in spring that will grow through the summer.

In this system, water is pumped from the reservoir to the plants, in most cases through 1/2-inch plastic pipe. A spaghetti line is attached to the pipe to feed and water each plant. The watering cycle is controlled by a digital timer that turns the pump off and on. It is easy to program these timers to water for a short cycle once a day, when plants are small, or when the weather is cool. It's also easy to give the marijuana as much water as necessary during the warm months of rapid growth. Digital timers can programmed for up to 12 cycles per day.

Drip line to greenhouse plants in the ground Photo: Sam Pedro

The hydro equipment used for greenhouse systems may differ from the smaller table systems. The pumps used in greenhouses often have a higher capacity because the water often has to be moved longer distances. Fifty to one hundred gallon per minute pumps are used by many

greenhouse growers. Reservoirs are also usually larger. Hundred gallon troughs or small swimming pools can be used.

Greenhouse Grows

Setting up a greenhouse grow is similar in many ways to other forms of hydro growing, although not exactly the same. The growing media that can be used in the greenhouse, for example, are the same as those outlined in chapter four. Greenhouse growers often use larger containers though because they often grow larger plants. Five-gallon containers are often used on full season marijuana. Besides offering more room for roots, the larger containers also prevent the plants from falling over when they get big. Other kinds of plant supports may still be needed. Growers using rockwool often use the larger slabs rather than cubes.

Excess humidity and heat are the limiting factors in many greenhouse grows.

Growers using the option of cultivating marijuana in the ground should condition the soil as deeply as possible. The soil can be conditioned with amendments, such as compost, ground bark, perlite or vermiculite, so that it is well aerated. Equal portions of soil and compost make a good mix. See the "grow hole" section in the next chapter.

Excess humidity and heat are the limiting factors in many greenhouse grows. Heat can limit growth during the long days of summer. Greenhouse temperatures can easily rise above 100°F during the summer months. Some growers use films or washes that will limit the amount of light and heat that can enter the greenhouse at this time of year. Good ventilation, of course, is a must, for cooling a hot greenhouse. A few growers use air conditioners to keep the temperatures tolerable, below 90°F.

High humidity can be a problem in greenhouses, especially in the fall when days are shorter and cooler. In this season greenhouses are often filled with plants, which adds much water to the air as the plants transpire. High humidity can lead to molding in flowering plants, or mildew if the marijuana is in vegetative growth. Marijuana can take relatively high humidity of 70-80% if a breeze is directed over the plants. Another solution is to raise temperatures

Greenhouse hydro flowers

with electric heat, or use a dehumidifier to both raise temperatures and lower humidity.

Greenhouse coverings can also "sweat" because of the difference between indoor and outdoor temperatures. Water from this sweating can drop on plants and cause mold. Some greenhouse kits are designed to direct this condensation away from plants. Pointing a fan at the roof of the greenhouse will also help mitigate this situation.

May the Force Be With You

Experienced marijuana growers know that you can grow out of season crops in a greenhouse. Uninterrupted darkness is the force than induces the species cannabis to form flowers. This is why marijuana flowers outdoors: the longer nights of autumn. Most strains of marijuana will fully flower whenever the day and night lengths are an equal, 12 hours. Early maturing varieties will begin to flower in shorter nights of as little as 10 hours.

For greenhouse growers this means that if marijuana is put in a greenhouse from late August to late March of the next year, it will immediately begin to set flowers. This includes small plants just a few weeks old. Some growers cultivate several crops during these months. Usually, plants are grown under electric lights and moved into the greenhouse when they reach the desired height. The cold, of course, is the limiting factor during winter months.

In the greenhouse, marijuana can be induced to flower at any time by artificially lengthening the night cycle. This is done with blackout shading used to artificially lengthen the night cycle. The shade cloth can be made of any material that prevents light from reaching the plants when the shades are closed. Six mil black plastic can be used to make an inexpensive shade. Some greenhouse supply stores sell material made specifically for this purpose.

A simple shading system can be opened and closed by hand. The shade is attached to cables or rope with clips so that it easily opens and closes around the plants. Since they have to be closed and opened at specific times each day, this kind of flower forcing is a chore. Growers can knock a couple of weeks off the flowering cycle by giving the marijuana very long nights of 14 hours. Plants should be shaded only from indirect light since the growing area can overheat if the shades are closed in direct sun.

Plants with Blackout Shades

Systems to automate the shading of marijuana can be set up with equipment made for household drapes. Small motors timed to open and close drapes at specific times are available. Check out home automation sites on the web to find these. These motors are made to work with drapery rods. Small motors will push and pull shades over a space about 4x10 feet, if the shades can move freely.

*Outdoor plants with automated
watering system*

Chapter 9

Outdoor Hydro

Outdoor guerrilla growers employed hydro growing techniques early on. In California, for example, having a reliable water source is a necessity in order to grow marijuana, because it seldom rains during the summer months. Once identified, the water has to be moved to the plants. Often, this is done with the same equipment employed by indoor growers - a drip hydro system. Ideally, the water will flow to the growing area by gravity.

Other hydro techniques employed by outdoor growers include conditioning the soil, either in the ground in "grow holes", or sometimes using large containers for the grow. Fertilizers are often supplied to the marijuana with soil amendments, or time-released fertilizers.

In other areas of the USA, local conditions dictate how much irrigation is necessary for a successful crop. In many areas, such as those east of the Mississippi River, a crop can live on the summer rains once it is established - at least in good years. In these areas, conditioned soil and some fertilizer may be all that is necessary to optimize a crop. Outdoors in these areas, the variety of marijuana grown is as important as the growing techniques used.

Two inch header line with 1/2 inch pipe connected

Varieties of marijuana have been developed that will mature outdoors as far north as Canada. The trick is getting hold of the right seeds. Though seeds are illegal in the USA, marijuana seed companies operate in several countries including Holland, Switzerland, and Canada.

Even so, a good clone, one adapted to local growing conditions, may be the best option. For our purposes, clones are rooted cuttings made from female plants. Having all female plants cuts the work of setting up the grow in half, compared to starting from seeds, when half the plants may be male. Good clones are derived from plants selected for attributes like high yield, early maturing date, taste, high, or bug and disease resistance in the location in which they will be grown.

Marijuana plants for outdoor grows are often started indoors under lights. If seeds are used, the plants can easily be sexed to determine whether they are male or female. Cutting the light cycle to 12 hours on, 12 hours off, for about 2 weeks will cause the plants to form small flowers on the main stem near the upper branch nodes of the marijuana. Once the sex is known and the males separated from the females or eliminated, plants are returned to long days (18-24 hours) or moved outdoors, if the time is right.

Marijuana grown outdoors will also indicate sex if it is started early enough. Marijuana starts to flower because of the day and night length. During spring many varieties of marijuana will produce a few small clusters of flowers. Though they won't amount to much, and will diminish as the long days of summer approach, they will indicate the sex of the plant.

When to start the marijuana outdoors is determined by the growing conditions, and the kind of garden the grower wants. Certainly growers want to wait at least until after the last frosts, when the ground warms up. Since marijuana grows so fast there is no real advantage to starting early. Big plants are more conspicuous, and often have to be pruned to avoid detection.

Small Plants Started Late

Growers who do want full-grown plants will start as early as possible. Keep in mind though, that the marijuana will flower at the same time in the fall even if planted in early July. Again, smaller plants are easier to hide.

It's getting hot out there, and I'm not just talking about cops and thieves. The atmosphere itself seems to be melting out into space. Besides getting free light, outdoor growers are getting increased carbon dioxide and ultraviolet light, as a result of global warming. Increased carbon dioxide makes pot and most other plants grow faster. Higher ultraviolet light levels have been shown to increase the potency of marijuana. For now, growing conditions are auspicious, at least for plants that get adequate water. That is, until we completely lay waste to the ozone layer.

The Water Source

When water is needed for the grow, water sources include streams, springs, ponds, and catchment. Catchment means collecting water when it rains and storing it for future use. The water can be delivered to the growing area by gravity flow, pumps, or with a combination of both. Solar and fuel powered pumps and other equipment such as water tanks, fertilizers or water lines are available at agricultural supply centers.

Water flows downhill by itself. This is the basis of gravity flow watering systems. Two kinds of systems are in common use. Near streams, a system can funnel water from an upstream location to the downstream grow. This is done with a collector that is submerged upstream. A pipe or hose is connected to the collector (sluice) or funneling device, and run to the growing area, which is located downhill from the water-channeling collector. Once at the growing area the water can be collected, or immediately directed to each plant with plastic pipe and spaghetti line used for drip irrigation.

A system like this runs all the time as long as the water source is flowing. Water-restricting devices like drip emitters can be used to slow down the flow of water to each plant. The spaghetti line, to which the drip emitter is attached, can be placed a couple of feet away from small plants and brought closer as the plant becomes established. Growers want to avoid soggy growing conditions which can slow plant growth.

In good, well-drained soil and dry growing conditions, a constant flow system may be just the thing. If the growing area gets too wet you can easily shut it off for a while. It's usually pretty easy to get more control on a system like this by adding a reservoir or water holding tank to the system. Battery operated timing devices are available that will turn the system off and on.

Gasoline powered pump drawing water from a pond

Automated watering cycles are set up using a water tank and an automatic valve to turn the water on and off. The modified drip system, without drip emitters, uses a spaghetti line to bring water to each plant. The Rainmatic®, by Nelson is the device often used to control this system. They have a web site but this piece of equipment is easy to find. It is available at most regular gardening stores. It is made for turning water on and off in the home garden. The Rainmatic® connects to ordinary 5/8 inch garden hose.

With the automatic valve the grower can control both how much water goes into the reservoir and how much is released. In the case of water coming in from a stream, one valve is installed before the reservoir and keeps it full. Another valve is attached to the bottom of the reservoir and releases water periodically to the plants. If a solar pump is used to fill the reservoir from a spring or other water source, it's easy to control how much water is coming into the water tank. Simply move the solar collectors to adjust the flow. Too much water? Move the collectors to a shadier location. Too little? More sun.

Outdoors, a water tank can be made out of just about anything. A thirty-gallon trash-can will supply a few plants. Then there are watering tanks for livestock, which can hold up to hundreds of gallons. There are also swimming pools of all sizes. Reservoirs can also be fashioned by laying down several layers of plastic in a depression in the ground or a crevice in a rock.

The size of the water tank needed depends both on the size of the grow, and how easy it is to hide. The tank also has to be above or on the same level as the growing area in order for gravity flow to work. Water tanks should have a cover to keep out debris, and also to prevent insects like mosquitoes from spawning in them.

If a gasoline pump has to be used for filling the reservoir, a large reservoir is indicated. These pumps are noisy and should be run as infrequently as possible.

Water is released periodically from the reservoir to the plants through the timing device. It is connected to drip line and spaghetti tubing. As was mentioned, drip emitters are not usually used. This helps prevent clogging of the water lines.

How not to water. Wetting foliage can lead to mold and mildew problems.

Hydro growing usually means using several shorter watering cycles, rather than watering deeply every few days. But outdoors in good soil, marijuana will put down a deep taproot. Deep, intermittent waterings, when the plants are young, will help establish a good, deep root system. In general, soils that don't drain well, like clay, will benefit from shorter watering cycles rather than a real soaking. A marijuana plant that sets deep roots can survive for a couple of weeks without water. Of course, marijuana that survives is different from plants that thrive.

Watering systems are used for lessening the number of trips to the growing area as much as for keeping the marijuana in prime condition. Local weather conditions will determine how much or little irrigation is needed. A system can be shut off in rainy periods and activated in drought conditions. Irrigation makes it much more likely the marijuana will make it to harvest, whatever the weather may bring.

The Grow Hole

Marijuana grows well in containers outdoors but because of the remote locations where marijuana is often grown, hauling soil may be unfeasible. Conditioning the soil in the growing area may be the best option.

If you can do containers, a drip system with spaghetti line to each container is easy to set up. The big advantage of containers is that they can be moved to take best advantage of the sun. Containers of five gallons or more are used on full-grown plants. The container and growing media have to be heavy enough to prevent large plants from falling over.

In the ground, marijuana thrives in a well-drained, sandy loam of a slightly acid pH. Not that you are likely to find this kind of soil in the forests where marijuana is often grown clandestinely. More often, growers encounter shallow soils with hardpan (clay) not far down. Clay soils aren't all bad. They often contain a lot of nutrients although seldom much nitrogen. Clay soils also hold a lot of water even though they can crust over which makes water penetration difficult.

Clay soils need to be broken up and conditioned to keep them from clumping. This keeps the soil open to both air and water penetration. You could haul in some lightweight materials like perlite or styrofoam beads to condition heavy soils. Or you can gather materials in the area. Sand, pebbles, leaf litter or twigs are effective soil conditioners. Pine needles shouldn't be used in large amounts because of pH and other potential toxicity problems. Clays can be mixed with an equal volume of soil conditioners.

Clay soils are best worked when wet. It can be difficult to dig after clay dries out. A dry growing area can be intermittently flooded for a couple of days until the water finally penetrates, then dug. Digging a foot into the hardpan will help assure the marijuana forms a good root system. Some growers condition the soil soon after the spring thaw, and plant later on. Cultivated areas are often left in a natural looking state so they don't pique the curiosity of hikers or helicopters.

Sandy soils are often well-drained and deep, making marijuana cultivation relatively easy.

Soil amendments for both pH adjustment and plant nutrition can be added once the hard pan is loosened and conditioned. Time-released fertilizers are often used to feed the marijuana. They release nutrients over time and work fairly well.

Sandy soils are often well-drained and deep, making marijuana cultivation relatively easy. Sand, for instance, is sometimes used as a hydro growing media indoors. Sandy soils usually drain rapidly and have low nutrient levels. These conditions can easily be supplemented with a hydro system.

The other soil types likely to be encountered outdoors are silts or mucks. These soils are made up of a high percentage of decayed organic matter and mud. They are often nutrient-rich but have lousy air penetration. Often, these types of soils indicate the area may flood in spring or after heavy rains.

Like clays, silts need conditioning to be a viable growing medium. These soils are usually easy to mix compost with and work. If area does have the potential to flood, mounds of up to 1 1/2 feet above ground level can be fashioned. This will help the marijuana withstand some high water. If an automatic watering system is used it should be shut down in rainy weather.

Mound gardening is a variation of early hydro gardening dating back as far as the Aztecs in Mexico. They constructed floating gardens, in the shallow areas of the lake surrounding Mexico City. Huge receptacles were built and filled with silt from the lake bottom and compost. The gardens eventually became permanent filled areas of the lake, as plant roots grew down into the water and anchored the garden to the lake floor.

I haven't heard of any growers doing a floating hydro marijuana garden, but it is certainly possible. Cagey outdoor growers have used just about every trick in the book to bring in a crop. Reports of growers using flower forcing techniques to bring in very early crops, or of growers hoisting marijuana plants up into trees to avoid detection, are not ficticious.

Once the marijuana is growing well and watering is squared away, growing is pretty laid back. The watering system has to be maintained, and a little fertilizer may be added to keep the plants lush. Marijuana plants may also be pruned to keep them from getting too large and to take best advantage of the available light. Plants are also pruned help the marijuana blend into the surrounding vegetation. Some growers prune lower branches, which are not getting much light and are not likely to produce many flowers.

As the marijuana begins to flower, many growers remove the large fan leaves on the main stalk where the plant branches. By removing these large leaves more light will reach the flowering sites. It will also make the plants somewhat less detectable. Fan leaves turn yellow as a first sign that the marijuana is becoming undernourished. If this is happening, give the plants a hit of fertilizer before removing the leaves.

Hunter-gatherer types should be aware of the habits and habitat of other animals and plants when setting up an outdoor grow. Poison oak and poison ivy occupy many forests. You wouldn't want to disturb certain reptiles either. It's a good idea to read up on the habitat in your area. Fencing, for example, may be needed to keep stoner deer or even moose from consuming the marijuana plants. You'll need to spend a lot of time in the forest to bring in an outdoor crop.

Way Ripe

Chapter 10

Hydro Harvest

The endgame for the marijuana grower is to bring the crop to harvest. Indoors, the marijuana can be grown from start to finish in 3 months or less. Some outdoor crops are cultivated for 6 months or more. The flowering sequence is always set off in the same way, by the number of hours of darkness the plant receives.

Flowering starts slowly, and the marijuana continues to grow rapidly. A couple of weeks into the process, a few small flowers appear on the main stem near the top of the plant. Growers call these indicator flowers, because they are used to determine the sex of the plant, especially when a crop is grown from seed.

Drying room with dehumidifier

Soon after the indicator flowers appear, the marijuana begins to rapidly set flowers. The number of fingers on each leave begins to decline as the plant forms flower calyxes along the branches and on the top of the main stem. Most of the flowers form in a few weeks although they are small and immature.

Soon each calyx, which would hold a seed if there were male plants around, swell as if they had been fertilized. The calyxes are covered in a clear crystalline resin, the sweet drug glands of the marijuana plant. These small, bulbous capitate glands expand as the flowers ripen. The fluid within them changes color from clear to amber, as thoughts of sugarplums dance through the grower's head.

The flowering sequence takes from 5 to 8 weeks, and on a few varieties longer. The early maturing varieties of marijuana are a wonder, and have rapidly expanded the outdoor growing range of the marijuana plant to the far north. Indoors, plants that mature quickly allow more crops to be grown. Most likely, these varieties of marijuana are the result of hybrid plant breeding being done in the tolerant countries of Canada, Holland, and Switzerland. Usually hybrid seed is suitable for only one or two crops although clones selected from a crop can be propagated indefinitely.

When exactly to pick the marijuana flower is a subject of hot debate. Lovers of sweet sinsemilla will pick while the drug glands are still clear, just before they turn amber. Those who subscribe to the epithet, "If you don't cough, you don't get off", let plants go as long as possible. If the flowers ain't molding they ain't harvesting.

First flowers on plant indicating it is female.

Dry Up

You have to harvest sometime and when you do, how the marijuana is dried and manicured will affect the taste and how long the flowers can be stored. How well a joint stays lit is also a result of how well the marijuana has been dried.

Once the ritual sacrifice of cutting down the virgin marijuana crop is complete, the plants are manicured to remove leaf, and dried as soon as is possible. Plants are easiest to manicure while the leaves are still turgid and protrude away from the flowers. How much leaf is cut away from the flowers is often determined by the variety of marijuana being grown. Indica varieties have leafy flowers that are highly resinous. Much of the resinous leaf is left on the flowers. Sativa flowers often take a closer cut during manicuring. The leaf on Sativa flowers can be harsh smoking.

Most growers prefer scissors with short blades and handgrips that accommodate all the fingers for manicuring the harvested marijuana flowers. These kinds of scissors are also useful in the grow room for pruning plants and taking cuttings.

A slight cure, which removes some of the chlorophyll from the flowers, will also enhance flavor.

If the marijuana can't be manicured right away, hang the marijuana plants up until you can get to them. Avoid crushing the delicate flowers, as this will make it more difficult to dry them properly.

When the marijuana is manicured, cut the branches away from the main stem. Also cut the large terminal bud from the top of the plant. The leaf is then trimmed around the flowers. Large flowers are usually hung to dry. Smaller flowers can be dried on plastic screens so that air can flow around them. The object of drying the marijuana is to get it into a smokable form by removing water from the flowers.

A slight cure, which removes some of the chlorophyll from the flowers, will also enhance flavor. No special methods are needed to cure the flowers. Simply pile up the flowers in a low pile when they are almost dry. Then leave them to dry for a couple more days until fully dry.

Low humidity levels of 40% aid in the drying of marijuana. The flowers will dry in higher humidity, but the process will take longer. Air movement and heat, 70F, will help dry the marijuana if the weather is wet and humidity is high. Drying the marijuana releases water into the air, which should be moved out of the drying area, especially if large amounts of flowers are being dried. A dehumidifier in the drying area can assure that flowers are dried at optimum humidity levels.

Molding of the flowers is what growers try to avoid while the plants are in late flowering through the drying process. Molding occurs during cool wet weather and can spread rapidly. Molds literally eat away the flowers and spread through the crop by the spores they release. Marijuana is often harvested as soon as any mold is detected. Mold spores can be killed by placing the infected flowers in a microwave oven for a minute or two before they are dried.

Leaf can also be dried. Although the leaf can be quite potent, particularly that manicured from flowers, it is not usually smoked because of its harsh flavor. More often, the leaf is used to make baked goods. Growers with lots of leaf sometimes use hash-making machines to remove the drug containing glands from the leaf.

Index